When Faiths Collide

Blackwell Manifestos

In this new series major critics make timely interventions to address important concepts and subjects, including topics as diverse as, for example: Culture, Race, Religion, History, Society, Geography, Literature, Literary Theory, Shakespeare, Cinema, and Modernism. Written accessibly and with verve and spirit, these books follow no uniform prescription but set out to engage and challenge the broadest range of readers, from undergraduates to postgraduates, university teachers and general readers – all those, in short, interested in ongoing debates and controversies in the humanities and social sciences.

Already Published

When Faiths Collide

Martin E. Marty

Blackwell
Publishing

BLACKWELL PUBLISHING
350 Main Street, Malden, MA 02148-5020, USA
9600 Garsington Road, Oxford OX4 2DQ, UK
550 Swanston Street, Carlton, Victoria 3053, Australia

First published 2005 by Blackwell Publishing Ltd

3   2005

Library of Congress Cataloging-in-Publication Data

Marty, Martin E., 1928–
When faiths collide / Martin E. Marty
p. cm. — (Blackwell manifestos)
Includes bibliographical references and index.
ISBN 1-4051-1222-0 (hard : alk. paper) — ISBN 1-4051-1223-9 (pbk. : alk. paper)
1. Religious pluralism. I. Title. II. Series.

BL85.M32 2004
201′.5—dc22
2004008396

ISBN-13: 978-1-4051-1222-2 (hard : alk. paper) — ISBN-13: 978-1-4051-1223-9 (pbk. : alk. paper)

A catalogue record for this title is available from the British Library.

Set in 11.5/13.5 pt Bembo
by Graphicraft Ltd, Hong Kong
Printed and bound in the United Kingdom
by TJ International, Padstow, Cornwall

The publisher's policy is to use permanent paper from mills that operate a sustainable forestry policy, and which has been manufactured from pulp processed using acid-free and elementary chlorine-free practices. Furthermore, the publisher ensures that the text paper and cover board used have met acceptable environmental accreditation standards.

For further information on
Blackwell Publishing, visit our website:
www.blackwellpublishing.com

To Laurence O'Connell

who in our fifteen years of work together
contributed to healing among the religions and
manifested the hospitality to people of many faiths
for which this book calls people to undertake risks.

Contents

Acknowledgments

The hosts at scores of universities and colleges where I first presented some of the ideas in this book have been gracious, the responding faculty and audiences helpful, and I thank them. Harriet Marty, as always, was of assistance in many ways and stages, and Micah Marty, my literary partner, photographed the cathedral window that appears on the cover. I am grateful to both wife and son.

Martin E. Marty

1

Religious Strangers as Menaces

The collisions of faiths, or the collisions of peoples of faith, are among the most threatening conflicts around the world in the new millennium. They grow more ominous and even lethal every season. Lulled as many in the West are when their neighbors and fellow citizens appear to be religiously indifferent and genially tolerant, they overlook trends that threaten the fabric of serene life everywhere.

These collisions occur when two communities of faith which are strangers to each other have to share the same space and resources or when two factions within a faith community become estranged. My thesis is that the first address to these situations should not be the conventional plea for tolerance among them, but is rather a call that at least one party begin to effect change by risking hospitality toward the other. The root *hospitāre* is "to receive a stranger," and *hospitālis*, is "of or befitting the reception of strangers." Conversation and interplay follow the acts of reception; both are full of risk.

Macro- and Micro-Levels

The collisions occur on both the macro- and the micro-levels. Macro-level conflicts usually issue in bloodshed. In India, Hindus fight Muslims. In Nigeria, Muslims in the north and Christians in the south fight over future dominion in that troubled nation. In Israel/Palestine, Muslims and Jews are in lethal combat. In Northern

1

Ireland, Protestants and Catholics war with each other. In the former Yugoslavia, Orthodox Christians and Muslims were recently killing each other. In these and other cases, religion inspires, exacerbates, or justifies conflicts that often also involve ethnicity, territory, revenge, and political ideology.

When Faiths Collide deals mainly with collisions that affect or occur within those societies or nations whose polities can be called republican, democratic, liberal, or free. Conflicts that occur in tyrannical or theocratic polities demand other kinds of addresses, though the presence of these does color much of what happens in nations that enjoy religious freedom.

Dealing with liberal societies, however, can no longer be done in the luxurious experience of protection from illiberal polities and agents. In the middle of the twentieth century theologian Reinhold Niebuhr could still speak of the United States as a gadget-filled paradise suspended in a hell of international insecurity. The intrusion of murderous fanaticism on September 11, 2001 symbolically cut the cord by which this "paradise" had been suspended, and actually plunged the United States into the world of insecurity that most people in most nations in most ages have experienced.

That new circumstance has broken open the cocoon of isolation and shattered the carapace of apparent security that citizens took for granted. These had resulted from awareness of the nation's physical distance from much turmoil, thanks to two wide oceans to the east and west and friendly neighbors to the north and south. Now the boundaries were obliterated between the "safe" world, where religions prospered in a setting in which religious tolerance prevailed, and the "unsafe" world, where religious intolerance and interfaith aggression dominated.

If once Americans could look on at collisions of faiths and sit back with the self-assurance that "it can't happen here," they do not regard as alarmist the expressions or actions of those who discern trends that would not only subject the nation to religious terrorism from without, but also to the subversion of the culture of tolerance by resentful and aggressive movements from within. It is with awareness

2

of that porousness of boundaries and the fragility of the structures of free societies that we write. At the same time, most of the diagnoses and suggestions reflect a scene in which conversation and counter-intolerance are legally protected and can be civilly encouraged.

On the micro-level, faiths collide within domestic, usually national settings. Some of the collisions result from the fact that groups of people in a nation at peace who share a faith with others who are at war somewhere else identify with these spiritual kin. Tensions at home result. Thus some Muslims in France, Germany, the United Kingdom, or the United States are in sympathy with Muslims on far away battlefronts, and this connection creates disruption. Through their partisan devotion to Israel some Jews are connected by a constitution with fellow citizens of other faiths or political stripes who are themselves sympathetic to Muslims and in some instances Christian Palestinians. On occasion Catholics in the United States support Catholic militants in Northern Ireland, and some Protestant fundamentalists create stirs there through their support of fundamentalist Unionists.

More often faiths collide when population shifts occur. Western European nations who desired the presence of Arab refugees to do hard work welcomed many Muslims, whom the Germans call "guest workers." Some citizens have often subsequently had difficulty finding ways to cope with the faiths of these newcomers. Also, thanks to migrations within a nation, large areas of European and American cities experience sudden population shifts. People on the move, sometimes within groups, bring their portable faiths with them. They then create or experience abrasion in encounter with those who have long been on the scene. Politicians often exploit such situations of change, playing as they can on worries of long-time citizens who are wary of strangers. Or they choose to aggravate the fears of newcomers who experience prejudice and harassment.

The landscape where these micro-level situations develop is not littered with dead bodies. One may on occasion see some defacing of mosques or synagogues, torching of Christian churches, or spewing of hatred by intense groups who invoke their God. Often, we

3

become aware of the stigmatizing of school children who are not immediately at home in the cultural patterns established by old majorities. While such scenes are not lethal, they do disrupt civil peace. They distract citizens from tasks that they might otherwise be undertaking to address other problems that whole societies face. They set neighbor against neighbor and deprive both of opportunities to take up citizen responsibilities.

These conflicts present problems to which there can be contentious but still in the end some peaceful address. They differ from some macro-versions, wherein the potentials of military counter-attack or other circumstances are so dangerous that peacemakers cannot risk entry onto their no-man's-lands. However, not to address the micro-situations that *are* addressable is to risk seeing domestic citizen groups increasingly identifying with their bloodletting fellow believers in battle zones far away.

Strangers: Here Be Monsters

To establish positive relations it is necessary for people to stop demonizing strangers, immigrants, and those who are religiously different, who appear to many of them to be monstrous.

Hartmann Schedel inscribed "Here Be Monsters" – *haec incoluerunt monstra* – on his map wherever he dealt with the unknown world. In his *Liber Chronicarum* of 1493 Schedel depicted the earth as he imagined it was after the Flood described in the book of Genesis. Jerusalem lay at its center, surrounded by Asia, Europe, and Africa. Medieval travelers had brought back reports of monstrous creatures about which they heard or concerning which they made up tales. Since these lived beyond the margins of the recognized world, Schedel placed them on the margins of his map. He depicted a man with an umbrella-foot, a person with a dog's head, and creatures lacking heads but bearing faces on their breasts. Here he was citing ancients, Pliny and Strabo. The cartographer accompanied these with images of a man who had six arms, a centaur, a cyclops, a hermaphrodite, a person with a giant underlip, and another with ears that hung to the waist.

These monstrous figures serve as metaphors for the unfamiliar, strange, and often menacing faiths that today are in collision. Many Europeans and North Americans, finding these threats to be remote, often underestimate the power and potential of such faith communities among the so-called world religions.

With good reason some are learning to adjust their visions and are beginning to determine how they will relate to the rest of the globe. In a world of 6.2 billion people, 2 billion are identified with Christianity, 1.25 billion with Islam, 836 million with Hinduism, 367 million with Buddhism, and 15 million with Judaism. These are but five of some 10,200 "distinct religions" known to today's mapmakers and chroniclers.[1]

In Schedel's day there were not only ominous figments of imagination but also real monsters, though not always religious in character. Pirates threatened the sea-lanes of the travelers on whose narratives he depended. Hostile people warred against each other and on the traders and explorers who invaded their space.

As the travelers came to know and deal with strangers, these did not all turn out to be monstrous. Instead, they often served as trailblazers, translators, and trading partners. Some of them had even created and inhabited cultures that welcomed strangers.

In the contemporary world, the unfamiliar strangers also are not always monsters. Not everyone in all societies wakes up every morning having to be cautious about the faiths of others, though in the age of terrorism ever more of them have reason to do so. Many non-religious people or those who are apathetic about faith and faiths, simply express hope that a growth in religious indifference and secularism can serve the human race in positive ways. Others make efforts to keep intense religious communities at a distance and do their best to ignore them.

More alert citizens of the world are at work attempting to effect polities and policies in which conflicting religions can learn to coexist and even cooperate with each other. Along with their formal efforts it is important to note the reservoirs of good will among ordinary people who, in the course of their daily lives, have learned to establish familiar and friendly relations with those who make up communities other than their own. They overcome strangeness and dispel the fear they might have associated with it.

Any inventory of forces at work today, however, will reveal that the conflict of faith communities who regard each other as monstrous has become the most volatile and often militant spiritual, or anti-spiritual, eruption in the world. Around the globe people gather into convulsive movements in which they define themselves over against others, usually in the name of God.

As if they did not experience enough conflict among themselves, many who long considered themselves remote from the worst are finding that there really are monsters "out there" in a world where the margins of their mental maps are no longer so remote. Where once pirates were the horrors, terrorists now cast shadows that menace everyone else. Most of these terrorists act in the name of some religion or other. Modern weaponry in the hands of terrorists has given potential victims reason to feel henceforth and forever insecure. Mass media of communication inform and stimulate modern imaginations about these monsters and monstrosities.

Faiths as Communities in Collision

The word "faiths," as mentioned, refers to communities of those who believe and behave in particular patterns because of the way that together they interpret human existence. So people may speak of the several faiths that make up a society. Ordinarily, people do this in response to what they experience as the transcendent, the supernatural, or the supra-human. While millions of them may respond independently of everyone else and in highly individualist ways, the majority of seekers and those who practice faiths grow up in or form communities where in common with others they can make response to the sacred.

Headlines and prime time television images serve as daily reminders that these faith communities often come into collision. "Colliding" means that strangers "come together with solid or direct impact." Why they do so, we will argue, has much to do with the way each perceives the others as strangers and hence as menaces to their beliefs and ways of life.

What they do about the strangeness is the subject of several chapters of this book. Many develop strategies associated with pluralism both to account for the way these communities are strangers to each other and for the way many are able to relate positively to each other. I shall advocate the theory and practice of hospitality, with all the risks that accompany it.

Central to all the argument is the observation that strangers so often come as or appear to be menaces. They may be strangers in a physical sense when they intrude on territory others have claimed. Members of one community believe that they have a right to claim that they alone belong in a privileged or unique way in a particular place. The communities may also be strangers in spiritual senses, coming at each other with clashing ideas, narratives, and intentions.

The reference to a particular place indicates that the menace of the stranger within a pluralistic polity involves boundaries and territories, usually of a national character. Most discussion of issues relating to pluralism deal with such bounded realities: Canada and Tibet together do not make up a pluralistic complex. Quebec, the Maritimes, and the rest of Canada, however, do.

In a maverick and chancy take on the etymology of "territory," William E. Connolly roots it in "terror":

> *Territory*, the *Oxford English Dictionary* says, is presumed by most moderns to derive from *terra*. *Terra* means land, earth, soil, nourishment, sustenance; it conveys the sense of a sustaining medium that fades off into indefiniteness. People, you might say, feel the claim the land they belong to makes upon them . . . But the form of the word *territory*, the *OED* says, suggests something different from the sustenance of *terra*. *Territory* derives from *terrere*, meaning to frighten, to terrorize, to exclude. And *territorium* is "a place from which people

are warned" . . . To occupy territory, then, is both to receive susten-
ance and to exercise violence. To become territorialized is to be
occupied by a particular identity.[2]

Connolly engages in a bit of verbal sleight of hand here. The *OED*
says right off that the etymology linking "territory" to *terrere* is questioned, and most dictionaries do not make such a link. However,
research on the subject of territory and on protection by those who
occupy it is ample and convincing. "Territorialized" people do not
welcome the unfamiliar, the strange, the strangers, be they immigrants,
refugees, exiles, displaced persons, new homeowners as neighbors,
marital partners, schismatics, heretics, traitors, beguilers, and many
other variants, each of whom may bring their different faiths with
them.

The vision of this scene as described may seem Hobbesian. That
is, each person or group appears to be suspicious of and even hostile
to the other, in an each-against-all situation. This is not – or need
not be – the case. They frequently do cooperate with each other and
some welcome agencies that work to reconcile those who might be
in conflict. Citizens who enjoy a liberal governmental polity can allay
the suspicion of strangers or reduce their menace using numerous
approaches, some of which we shall later explore.

Religious Strangers as Particular Menaces

The roots of "menace" are in the Old French word *menacier* and
behind that the "OF-F noune" *menace*. Underlying that word is the
Latin *minācia*, from the adjective *minax*. And even further behind
those are words like *minae*, which referred to projecting points or
pinnacles. They thus connote anything that projects or overhangs,
the way a roof or a rock overhangs. Such a projection threatens to
fall on the unprotected. Strangers, in this picture, are projected into
situations and thus they disturb. The dictionaries stress that to menace
is always seen as intending to inflict evil, or it threatens with an

indication of probable evil to come. But strangers do not have to remain menacing. Contemporary pluralistic societies are made up of peoples and groups who started out as strangers to each other.

The idea of addressing estrangement and the situation of strangers in a hospitable spirit and with the intention to invite positive inter-action developed through my long career of dealing first with diversity in North American life. Monitoring and reporting on the ways dif-ferent religious bodies and faith communities related to each other alerted me to the need to understand how factions within denomina-tions or religions had become estranged. More recently, though a historian of American religion, concerned to chronicle this most pluralistic society, I was jostled into dealing with global issues that bear on America.

One decisive incident in the United States that altered the circum-stances for interpreters of American religion was the liberalization of immigration laws by the Congress in 1965. The number of strangers increased dramatically. Coming from Asia, Africa, and Latin America with religion in hand and mind, they often represented a problem to those who claimed prior rights of belonging, who cherished their place of privileged possession of the country, and boasted a particu-lar European-American heritage that they did not wish to share.

Through all those years, though Americans have been described as an unsettled people, many had shaped and settled into formerly homogeneous neighborhoods or regions. Then, typically, as African Americans moved to metropolitan inner cities, white citizens often moved out to suburbs, where they put down stakes and instantly claimed rights that they felt were proper for those who have belonged somewhere longest. The race, ethnicity, and religion of the urban newcomers who were displacing them and were prompting their flight to the suburbs loomed as menaces. Yet before long, many of the suburbs to which the whites had earlier escaped also began to become home to Asian, African, Native, and Hispanic Americans, most of them religious. Their skin color and expressions of faith were unsettling to those who thought of the suburbs as the place for their exclusive belonging.

9

Especially in the decades after 1965, housing court agendas revealed a nation struggling with the reality of pluralism, while its academies dealt with what came to be called multiculturalism. I was jostled out of my comfortable studies of religion in American history and was called to study collisions of faiths on international levels as several academies, foundations, and associations asked me to direct or co-direct some projects, most of them global in scale. These included work on militant religious fundamentalisms, religious ethnonationalisms, population–migration–development, and the religious dimensions of globalization ethics. I participated in but did not direct one on the religious issues in human rights. Meanwhile, some comparative studies on the American scene included assignments to direct or co-direct projects on public religion, civility in religious discourse, and conflict over constitutional freedoms and religion.

By then, ten years into my series of assignments to foray into international and other comparative studies, the line of distinction between the United States and everywhere else had, for me, become quite blurred. Older American claims of exceptionalism and illusions that the United States would not experience the effects of conflicts elsewhere came to be questioned. Global menaces to American security reached the psyche of all citizens after the terrorist acts in New York and Washington on September 11, 2001. These brought the activity of monstrous strangers to American shores and gates. Since religion was now central to foreign policy and military action, the United States, while seeking to counter terrorist threats overseas, found itself needing education about the faiths of strangers.

Out of such experiences and to nurture the curiosities they inspired, I am in this manifesto reporting on a search for generic categories which can help provide understandings of specific challenges and the beginnings of engagements over them. All the conflicts we studied or represented had distinctive features, but we also saw some things in common. One of them is central in this book: the relation of those who "belong" in a place or a faith tradition and those they regard as strangers. Reflection on that commonality can inform specific inquiries concerning the interplay of people who feel they

belong and strangers wherever they may be and whatever is the
immediate cause of their abrasions.

The Intention of a Manifesto

When Faiths Collide appears in a series of Blackwell Manifestos. The
conventions of scholarly writing lead authors to be restrained in
the judgments and proposals they make. This is especially the case
with historians. Now comes the assignment to write a manifesto. "In
this new series, major critics make timely interventions to address
important concepts . . . ," aiming their books at those "interested in
ongoing debates and controversies in the humanities." That description sounds calming and neutral enough, but lurking behind it is the
menacing dictionary definition and the public's sense of what a
manifesto is: "a written statement declaring publicly the intentions,
motives, or views of its issuer."

This issuer will not claim to have a solution to the problems of
strangers. No one does. I accept the challenge of contributing to the
conversation and passing on tentative suggestions in the spirit that
goes with a congenial vocational description, José Ortega y Gasset's
concept of the "civic pedagogue." Such a teacher is not the dis-
penser but the fellow learner. I hope to present readers with some
understanding of the zones where the religious meanings and intentions of strangers have become confused and heated, so that more of
them can, with me, come to explore understandings, options, and
alternatives we may previously have been overlooking.

If the invitation to write a manifesto is a call for a historian to
drop out of his or her conventional role and make proposals, in this
case we may also be willfully transgressing the boundaries of conventional manifestos. One expects them to reflect the outrage of the
authors; for example, against injustices or indifference on the part of
others. Most manifestos are polemical, tinged by tones of rage and
boldness when it comes to the proposal of alternatives to the way
things are, or appear to be. I have learned from and have respect for

11

such manifestos. We historians would have duller stories to tell if we could not unearth and report on documents in which the author's singleness of purpose combined with rashness was not evident.

The intent of this manifesto, however, purposely is of a different character. Moved less by outrage than by concern, if not fear, and moving toward a bid for conversation more than argument, I am dedicated to the ideal of inviting "the other" into the zone where common action can develop – and accepting invitations from others. Barking at them will drive them away and prevent me from under-taking the self-examination that the current analysis and proposal require.

Here, as in similar ventures, my colleagues and I are moved by the example of Spinoza, who averred that when he set out to explore complex human actions, he made a sedulous effort not to laugh, not to cry, not to denounce, but to understand. There may be laughable elements in the actions of agents here described, but this is not the place to deride. There definitely are phenomena that can induce crying and inspire denunciation, but my vocation, calling, and assignment is to try to understand and join others who share such a mission.

2

"Belongers" versus Strangers

Belonger. *Obs. Rare.* He who or that which belongs . . .

Stranger. 1. One who belongs to another country, a foreigner . . . an alien. 2. One who is not a native of, or who has not long resided in, a place.

(*Oxford English Dictionary*)

People who form communities devoted to belief in God, or who adhere to particular religious outlooks such as Buddhism that do not include God, often create problems for others. When they encounter people who revere other gods or hold to other outlooks, some of them become threats and challenges. Picture it: a person or group from an unfamiliar tribe or clan or nation arrives on an alien scene. Those who feel they alone have the right to belong in that territory display fear that the strangers will subvert their values. On the other hand, they may fear that strangers will try to proselytize, to win people away from such a group and threaten a community itself. In either case, hostility results.

Such interactions are not novelties. Historical records are full of accounts that show how regular and how threatening they have always been. Age-old patterns of migration, the acts of taking captives, being refugees, or establishing trade routes, found strangers brought to new locales. Foreign people time and again made their presence known and felt among those who regarded themselves as native. The epics of ancient Greece and the biblical accounts of the children of Israel being strangers in Egypt and Canaan, plus the classic stories of

13

seafarers and traders across ocean boundaries, demonstrate something of the power strangers have held in imaginations and policies.

Immediate and Mediated Strangers

In the past two centuries this situation has changed character, especially after the inventions that made rapid travel possible. Add to this the rise of economies that transcend the boundaries of the local more than once they did, and involve different groups of people with each other as part of globalization processes. Atop this, add mass media of communication. The inventions and deployment of instruments such as the wireless and the telephone and then of radio, television, and the electronically accessed web, have made it ever more difficult to keep strangers at a distance. A viewer or a reader today has a choice of virtually every kind of commercial, sexual, or religious image with the twist of a television dial or the turning of a newspaper page. In the blur of such imageries, some strange, often religious, signals will stand out as challenges.

Defenses against all the alien voices and images that are borne through mass communications have evoked many drastic responses. Once upon a time the walls of ghettos, the fences around slave quarters, or the natural boundaries set by mountains or rivers served as protection of local people and their values. They are less isolated now. Our studies of militant fundamentalisms around the world showed how it was mass media that evoked so many defensive strategies and provoked offensive tactics from those they attacked.[1] Non-fundamentalist observers of such fundamentalisms, by whatever name they were called, had long been invited to think of such very modern movements as "the old-time religion."

Members of such retro-movements, meanwhile, welcomed those kinds of stereotyping. It marked them with stigmata whose visibility promoted their own sense of identity and threw off guard those who opposed them. But by instinct or in stealth, it turns out, they themselves were learning to make use of such media of communication and

14

soon outpaced the efforts of their more moderate and less threatened neighbors. The images or voices of strangers thus served militant religious groups as well as the physical presence of any of them might do.

Even a quick survey of the media will provide evidence that movements in defense of one's own holy land and the rejection of strangers, which means of "everyone else," shows how the process develops. Thus, the Iranian revolution of 1978–9, the one that alerted much of the world to the power of these new movements, had been fostered in no small measure by the dissemination of tape recordings. They issued to and from followers of the Ayatollah Khomeini, who was in exile in France.

After Iran, outbreaks of terrorism elsewhere, often from people on the Islamic right, followed. These altered many features of geopolitics after the 1990s. Terrorists became most adept at using the web, the internet, to plot their activities. More mildly, in the United States, while moderate Roman Catholics, Reform and Conservative Jews, and mainstream Protestants fumbled and ordinarily failed to find focus in the use of radio and television, fundamentalist-like groups mastered them and won political power by such use. They often inconvenienced those who had held power.

For another example, American evangelist Jerry Falwell on occasion pointed to the access mass media had won and what were to his followers strange signals with which the mass communicators could penetrate every home. He would assert that during the Civil Rights Movement in the 1960s and 1970s the fundamentalists had hoped to keep their religion pure and untainted. Back then they therefore claimed it was sinful for Christian movements to express themselves in politics. By the time Falwell made that observation in the 1980s, circumstances had changed and movements of his sort found it necessary to reverse themselves. Now, he said, it was a sin for them *not* to enter the political sphere, there to fight off the influence of strangers. He defined as alien some secular humanists, liberal Christians, and purveyors of sex and violence in the media.

Leaders like Falwell rationalized their about-face, repeatedly explaining that earlier the leaders thought they could keep the world

15

of strangers at a distance. Thus, the excluded could not easily contaminate, pollute, or beguile the faithful. Now, however, mass media such as television made it impossible for anyone to block the signals of that world. Somehow the children of even the most disciplined families would find access to such signals, or the signals would find them. These held such enthralling power to shape outlooks on life that by the time parents tried to set examples or to instruct their own children, it was too late: they had been preformed and perverted by the alien influences.

For that reason, such fundamentalists reacted. They *had* to react. Our studies showed that the concept of reaction in response to the threat of the stranger was the most decisive element in turning classic conservatives, the orthodox, or traditionalists, into modern fundamentalists. Thus, in the United States, Orthodox Jews or the ultra-conservative Amish were not fundamentalist, did not call themselves fundamentalist, and nor did their neighbors, their friends and enemies, and scholars. They were simply for a longer time more successful than were others at living in enclaves or effecting disciplines that kept the media at some distance from their followers. The modern fundamentalists, as they progressively blended into the world of markets, the universities, and civil society, could not screen out those signals.

For such reasons, these fundamentalists and their counterparts among other nations followed two strategies. Some of them responded by becoming effective and alluring to large clienteles themselves. Thereupon their constituents, they reasoned, would find them attractive and would choose to screen out alien signals from the surrounding world. Others would undertake efforts to minimize the power or actually to block the signals of the strangers that came with media. Such undertakings could occur through voluntary boycotts, legal efforts to restrict what were regarded as blasphemous or pornographic representations, or, though not in the United States, engagement in terrorist activities to demolish the presses or transmission towers of those who, they claimed, were subverting their cherished and even only-true ways of life and ideologies.

The Alluring Stranger

Mention of fundamentalists needing to keep strangers at a distance because they are so alluring signals one of the more apparently contradictory features of the strangers' presence. They and other members of intense groups erect boundaries, create distance between themselves and others, not always because the stranger is abhorrent but because she may be beguiling. An extended figurative or metaphoric example illuminates this feature. In literature, the stranger presents herself so temptingly *because she is foreign* that the members of a defined community have to create taboos to keep her at a distance. They must condemn her if she is near, or put her away if she becomes an insider.

Almost by instinct I have spoken of the female stranger. Ancient and profound sacred literature suggests why this is the case. Gail Corrington Streete has isolated this character and her particular feature in *The Strange Woman: Power and Sex in the Bible*.[2] Streete tells how in the Deuteronomistic history of the people of Israel, writers after the exile needed an explanation of what had befallen them when the northern ten tribes fell and the southern two, Judah, were taken captive in Babylon.

> They found it in the non-Israelite women ("foreign women" or *nokriyyoth*) whom they blamed for causing Israelite and Judahite kings to follow "other" deities, causing an angry YHWH, the God of the Israelites, to take away that land that was their promised inheritance (Genesis 12:1–9) . . . Deuteronomy 7:3–4, a text composed or at least edited during the exile, expresses the fear that daughters given in marriage to non-Israelites, and non-Israelite daughters married to Israelite sons, will "turn away" the hearts of their husbands from YHWH to follow other deities . . . It is no accident that the infamous figure of the adulteress, the seducer of foolish young men, also called the "strange" or "outsider" woman (*'iššah zarah*) is also developed in this postexilic period as a seductive, lethal monster against whom the young men of Proverbs (chapters 1–9) must be warned.

When the men of Israel were accused of adultery, it was because they were seduced by those alluring "strange" women. "When they commit apostasy, the religious crime often spoken of as adultery, the same 'foreign' or 'strange women' are again responsible." In prophetic language, Israel as a whole engaged in sexual adventures with foreign women. Because they were then attracted to their foreign gods, God's people left YHWH behind as a kind of abandoned wife.

King Solomon took many wives and concubines. Because they were from enemy territory like Egypt, Moab, Ammon, Edom, and Sidon, they were able to "turn away his heart" from YHWH to foreign gods and their abominations. The combination of sex, sometimes only figuratively and metaphorically, and literal faithlessness in such texts indicates how potent the role of the strange woman as seductress was seen to be. She was the symbol of the lure also of other, strange, foreign faiths that were disruptive of the piety and power of those who belonged as members of tribes in the two kingdoms. Today, the religious stranger can seem seductive, and must be countered by guardians of a religious movement that would stand apart.

The Strangers, Beginning with the Self

The experience of estrangement or fear of the stranger can begin as close to home as the self. The self as stranger is at one end of a continuum that stretches from the most intimate to the national and international spheres. To study it means beginning with the idea of individuals being strangers to themselves, and then proceeding through community abrasions caused by immigration, through tribal[3] warfare around the globe, to terrorisms that cross all boundaries of nation or religion. The various meanings and roles of strangers differ vastly from each other along this continuum, depending upon where along this scale of intimacy and distance they are to be found. The search for what they have in common, however, rewards those who would understand what being a stranger means.

To begin at the beginning: before one speaks of even the strangers next door, it is necessary to promote self-awareness by focusing on the strangers at home, which means to see individuals as strangers to themselves. When alienation in its extreme form takes a psychic toll it produces the divided self, as seen in pathologies of schizophrenia or bipolar swings. In more moderate forms, alienation is apparent when in times of profound uncertainty or confusion about identity a person speaks of being a "stranger to myself." Becoming aware of the self-as-stranger may strike some readers as a strange place to start an inquiry, or an offbeat subject to include in a book dealing with strange others. Yet psychologists regularly point out that alienated individuals or groups are more likely to work out their insecurities on other groups than are those who have dealt with their self-estrangement and consequently improved their mental health.

Characteristically, we speak of alienation occurring as the result of experience in a cultural vacuum or wasteland, an estrangement from meaningful community. The experience of such estrangement results in aloneness, resentment, and hostility over against others. But there are many versions of being a stranger to one's self. If, as we shall argue, a way to address the stranger is, among other things, to manifest itself in hospitality, all this means that a person must overcome alienation before she can be open to the other. This inner exploration begins with probing until one comes to some discernment, based on partial answers to questions such as: Why have I been fearful, paralyzed, immobilized, or rendered apathetic? Why have I been unable to find perspective, to look at the other person or group in open ways? Further, what commitments have I made that lead me to have to be distanced from or suspicious of the religious stranger? If those who ask these questions have previously ignored or denied such, with new resolve they can explore resources for overcoming estrangement. They may find them especially when experiencing the true stranger.

Analysis of the way the self-estranged deals with "the other" has been stock-in-trade in the creative agendas of mid-century existentialists – figures such as Emanuel Mounier, Gabriel Marcel, and Viktor Frankl. A student of the three, William Blair Gould, has conflated their insights in an efficient paragraph:

> Mounier uses the term *estrangement*, but the word *alienation* better describes the separation of the self from others. *Alienation* conveys the sense of being threatened by a hostile environment, of being subject to conditions that are not understood and over which the person has no control . . . [The result, Marcel speaks of as] unavailability . . . the person is not "present" to the other. [Frankl speaks of the need to reach out:] Such reaching out involves risk − the bounding leap of self-transcendence − but it enables us to become fully human, to become free of the prison of our own ego so that we can be present to the other. In other words, we exchange *indisponibilité* for *disponibilité*, instead of retreating from the other, we choose to be a being-for-another. Alienation is replaced by interdependence, in which the freedom and responsibility of both persons are not only preserved but also enlarged.[4]

This replacement sounds almost romantically therapeutic, since it suggests that one can overcome estrangement from the self by dealing with estrangement from the other. Yet "the other" is not always "available" and does not come without problems for the reaching-out self. And that other is not off in Northern Ireland, on the West Bank, or in Tibet. He or she is near, in intimate range, inescapable, and a creator of problems to those who would undertake risks of relation.

Strangers Under Roof

Those whom we have seen as strangers to themselves encounter other strangers all through life, often in situations where their separate faiths have the potential of colliding. Some homey examples can serve. Thus, two roommates at a university, or as they pursue their careers, may not find it necessary to come to terms with or to settle all issues dealing with religion. This is so in part because their covenant may be casual, one even imposed by the school authorities who placed them in a dormitory room. For the other part, they make few commitments to each other beyond those required if their arrangements are to be civil. In any case, these tend to be temporary, less urgently to be resolved than in those situations that can last a generation or a lifetime. Still, such roommates can experience considerable stress over religion.

Cohabiting couples may treat personal and non-legal covenants as seriously as they would regard formal and legal commitments in marriage. They are more likely to have addressed the issue of two faiths under one roof than are those who have plunged into a relationship without giving thought to complexities. Some regard cohabitation as an experimental situation in which religious differences can be overcome or can lead to a break-up.

In religious communities, the most intense crisis occurs when couples marry across boundaries of faiths. Often, whole families become involved when couples contemplate religious "mixed marriages." In many cultures arranged marriages are powerful inhibitors against exogamy and thus cultural disruption: Hindu parents pick a Hindu spouse for their offspring. Thus they do what they can to ensure a marriage with partners in the same religious community and help keep a strenuous outsider at a distance. Jews in Europe characteristically married Jews. In the United States, though rabbinic law opposed it, many married non-Jews, crossing boundaries and introducing religious strangers into Jewish family connections.

Until the Second Vatican Council (1962–5) eased some of the strictures against intermarriage of Catholics and non-Catholics, marriages meant signing many covenants. Couples may still be expected to do this signing, but societal and religious institutional taboos have become less effective at enforcing the prohibitions.

Some who violate taboos or risk participation in marriages across religious and cultural boundaries may have resolved the crisis to their own satisfaction before the wedding day. Subsequently, however, many find that they run into hostility and suspicion among religious authorities who are called upon to bless the marriage. Or they experience unpleasant wedding receptions, as two family circles refuse to merge, and thereafter turn icy. Later, as a marriage matures, the love that led the couple at first to overcome religious differences may fail to continue to do so. Especially when the issue of bringing up children in one faith or the other or both comes up, new stresses appear. These distancings within a family that includes two or more faiths often continue all the way up to the time when families must determine which burial rites to follow.

These dire and depressing readings of situations sound like worst-case scenarios, and they may well be. They assume an intensity in commitments that is not always present in more religiously relaxed cultures. Mutual apathy, indifference, or lack of interest may prevail, thus lessening the role of religion as a factor in marital conflicts. More positively viewed, the press and electronic media often spotlight what the demographers reinforce with statistics: that in all kinds of nations and cultures, people make attempts to let love dictate the means chosen to overcome religious differences and to diminish the menace of the stranger under roof.

Even when couples or parents and children or others who have chosen intimacy or who cannot freely escape it share the same religious community, however, strangeness often menaces. A Reform Jew of liberal sensibilities might marry a partner who appears to be a spiritual kin. Later, he or she finds that the partner, a "like," then comes to differ in Orthodoxy, wants to make *aliyah* and head for Israel – with the children – and demonstrates thus how abrasive and disruptive life can be when someone near becomes estranged. The liberal Christians whose daughter at university rooms with and is converted by a conservative Charismatic and who then refuses to come home for the next holiday unless the whole family converts, or who treats the old circle of the family with condescension and hostility, regards her as the enemy under roof.

The Islamic community today is torn among those on the one hand who adapt to liberal societies and make accommodations to the culture, and on the other among those who revert to life in Muslim communities ruled by the laws of shari'ah. Distress enters the family circle. Philosopher Ernest Gellner observed at the time of the Iranian Shi'ite revolution in 1978–9 that many young women began wearing the *chador*, the veil, not because their mothers wore it but because their mothers did not. Grandmothers did, but mothers in their relative liberation had made some compromises. As a result, granddaughters often lacked an identity and in reaction acquired the identity of a militant religious adherent.

Perhaps for understandable reasons, more energy goes into efforts by marital counselors, psychologists, and religious authorities to address under-roof strangeness than into most other forms. Manuals on marriages across the lines of faith communities and studies of intergenerational adaptations are developed to address these situations. But their authors have only begun to offer positive ways to deal with such strangers. In any case, the problem of the stranger-to-the-self is on a continuum with that of the stranger under roof.

The Stranger Next Door, or Down the Street

The next zone where religion plays into the complex of human relations is where the stranger appears in the neighborhood. To get a grasp of the problem of the religious stranger in the neighborhood I am going to draw on insights from German sociologist Georg Simmel (1858–1918). He was particularly attuned to the issues represented by space, as when he studied "nearness and distance" in human relations. Two individuals or two social groups cannot occupy precisely the same space, so the issue of exclusivity arises. Simmel observed that the boundaries among groups are not necessarily natural, such as when a river or a mountain divides them. The barriers are usually social and, in some ways, artificial. Thus the line separating western Canada from the United States is not a natural one. Surveyors and mapmakers once established and recorded it. Yet people living on one side of it live by one set of laws and citizens on the other live with a different set. In a city, one can cross a street and move from a neighborhood in which Malaysians are prominent into one in which people of long-term British descent prevail. There need be no wall between them. Habit, custom, language, and religion will be agents that keep them separate. When a Malaysian family moves across that boundary it takes on the new status, that of the stranger. Thus it represents both threat and promise.

In an essay on "The Stranger," Simmel succinctly provided a framework for our whole inquiry.[5] Spatial relations, Simmel hastened to stress, "are only the condition, on the one hand, and the symbol, on the other, of human relations." He was interested not in the stranger who comes today and goes tomorrow but in the person who comes today and stays tomorrow. Such a stranger is not a wanderer, but a *potential* wanderer. He had the freedom to come and has a freedom to go.

> The stranger . . . is fixed within a particular spatial group, or within a group whose boundaries are similar to spatial boundaries. But his position in this group is determined, essentially, by the fact that he has not belonged to it from the beginning, that he imports qualities into it, which do not and cannot stem from the group itself.

This distinction is so important that we are going to isolate, recast, and consistently use it in what follows. On the one hand are the people who belong, who live in what Simmel speaks of along the lines of a host culture. Though they cannot truly have been there "from the beginning," they think of themselves as having been so, and we will call them, sometimes with a tinge of irony, the *belongers*. Not much for coining new words or usages, I do feel licensed to disinter honored words that have fallen out of usage in the course of the centuries. It is entirely appropriate and useful in the present context and can be of great aid in framing the polarity with which we shall work.

In addition to their sense of belonging because of their priority in occupying a place, those at home in a place who claim rights to it become irritated by foreigners because these aliens "import qualities . . . which do not and cannot stem from the group itself." Mark the word "qualities": it has much to do with religious belief and praxis.

The Turkish *Gastarbeiter* in Germany or the Mexican migratory worker who is on the scene in Minnesota only seasonally occupies a different position than does the member of either of those groups who prospers, purchases a house, and stays. Those around them who have long belonged to the community must somehow come to terms with that immigrant or settler, now citizen, whose qualities, especially in religion, may be unsettling.

Simmel accents a dialectic that is also a "unity of nearness and remoteness," something that is present in all human relations, as we noted when dealing with the individual as stranger-to-the-self or the one who relates to the stranger under roof. But the price of relations rises when the neighborhood is challenged: "in the relationships to [this stranger], distance means that he, who is close by, is far, and strangeness means that he, who also is far, is actually near." Remarkably, the stranger can thus be in a positive relation to those who were in place, assuming "a specific form of interaction."

With a witty and wise tweak, Simmel reminds us that the inhabitants of Sirius are not really strangers to us; they do not exist at all, being "beyond far and near." Like the poor and sundry "inner enemies," the stranger instead "is an element of the group itself." He becomes a full-fledged member, being an owner and a citizen, but is also outside the group and confronts it.

Simmel illustrates all this with reference to the particular trader who "settles down in the place of his activity, instead of leaving it again." The example about which he wrote early in the last century makes the point in a way that we now see to be chilling: "The classical example is the history of European Jews." The stranger is "no owner of soil," physically or figuratively. He may develop charm and significance but as stranger he is not an "owner of the soil." Those who remember the Nazi stress on "blood and soil" can be reminded of how group membership and exclusivity can go extremely wrong.

In a sense, "the proportion of nearness and remoteness" gives the stranger the character of objectivity. He or she "sees" what long-time belongers may not. The stranger represents the universal:

25

The stranger is close to us, insofar as we feel between him and ourselves common features of a national, social, occupational, or generally human nature. He is far from us, insofar as these common features extend beyond him or us, and connect us only because they connect a great many people.[6]

After the terrorist attacks of September 11, 2001, in many communities in Great Britain and the United States the Muslim neighbor who might previously have been at least grudgingly welcomed as a citizen and parent suddenly came under suspicion. Why? Because his membership in a global community of Islam made him "far from us," meaning far from the non-Muslim majority. In some cases, the common features of humanity came to be eclipsed and the Muslim was not typically seen as the owner of an electronics store or restaurant but perhaps as a supporter of a foundation that channeled funds to the terrorist organization al-Qaeda.

Simmel went further in analyzing the neighbor as stranger. "There is a kind of 'strangeness' that rejects the very commonness based on something more general" which should embrace both the party of longtime belongers and newcoming strangers. The perception of the "strangeness of origin" of the newcomers by the old timers can be abhorrent. In American cities where militant Muslims were reported to have threatened members of diplomatic, commercial, or religious communities from the West, exclusivity turned extreme. Some of such Muslims had been familiar neighbors, sometimes friends. But now their individuality was subsumed and they became potential targets as aggressive defenders of a place, because they came from an outside – that is, from a strangers' place.

This kind of distorted perception prevailed in the case of European Jews in the eyes of the Nazis before the Holocaust. No Jew was to be seen as an individual Jew. Simmel observed a century ago how to many non-Jews, all Jews had to be seen as members of a group, a people, and not as individual persons. "Strangers are not really conceived as individuals, but as strangers of a particular type;

26

the element of distance is no less general in regard to them than the element of nearness."

Startling to many formerly exclusive groups and residents of neighborhoods – some of them as large as the nation itself – has been the awareness that came to many people at the turn of the millennium as they regarded public education. This was an awareness that the stranger is connected by inheritance, kinship, memories, and religious commitment, to others who are "beyond far and near." When the stranger moves into the neighborhood, it is the local scene that bears the brunt of change.

Given adult concern for education of the young, this was most evident in nations and places where there is a large measure of local control of schools. What those in control perceived as local now took on an international, universal dimension. This change was evident when Canadian schools passed regulatory laws against children bringing weapons to public schools. In some provinces, Sikh boys came wearing a ceremonial knife, a practice to which their faith and community committed them. Similarly, Muslim girls would not shed the *chador* to participate in athletic and other activities where the school has historically dictated the garb to be worn. Why, some citizens asked, should ayatollahs a world away be free to interpret the laws of shari'ah and determine customs in Vancouver, British Columbia?

The local, the neighborhood about which we are speaking, is connected to the global scene in ways that the trader historically represented. Republicans swept into most major offices in many locales in the United States in 1993, early in the administration of President Bill Clinton. This devastation occurred in an "off-off-year election," one that did not bear the significance of biennial or quadrennial elections. The president counseled his party and the nation not to read too much into this vote. They should not see it as a repudiation of national administration policies. He quoted Congressman "Tip" O'Neill, who famously said that "all politics is local."

Soon after, *New York Times* columnist William Safire, no admirer of the president or the congressman, averred that for once he agreed with both: yes, all politics is local. But what the two had not discovered was that today the local *is* the national. What is fought out in school boards and other instruments that normally exercise local control is an extension of global issues. For more than a century, non-Roman Catholics were often suspicious of the Catholics who encroached on their once-exclusively Protestant space. This was so not because Catholics in any way lacked the qualities associated with good citizenship or exemplary family life. No, they were strangers because, as Simmel said, they had not belonged to the group "from the beginning," and religiously they might *potentially* "move on."

When religious warrants are used to justify differences, these differences grow ever more intense. When people consult and follow Kabbalah, the Qur'an, the Gospel of John, or the Upanishads they are in place to underscore their strangeness and to accent the dialectic of nearness and remoteness. This is so because they conceive of these books as bringing sacred messages that are inaccessible to all but believers. In his *Roman à clef* novel *A Simple Honorable Man*, Conrad Richter tells the story of a boy whose father in mid-life decided to become a Lutheran minister. One day he heard the father rehearsing for a baptism. The boy heard the footsteps of his pacing senior, and the mumbling of rehearsed words. His father was quoting the baptismal ritual, talking about how evil an infant was at birth, how doomed the baby was because of this inherited evil, apart from baptism and faith. The Richter boy asked: how could donning a black suit and reading out of a little black book of sacred rites so change his humane and gentle father into someone who was ready to tell parents how evil and doomed their baby was?[7]

In neighborhoods, the possession and use of a different sacred book, a testimony of divine revelation, by the stranger who is a newcomer can be especially unsettling to those who insist that they and their book and its revelation only have a rightful place.

28

Strangers in Conflict

Conflict results. To throw consistent light on that result, I am going to draw again on Georg Simmel, who was also expert on social conflict, but this time to read him as mediated by Lewis A. Coser.[8] Like Simmel and like me in the development of this book, Coser could see positive values in the challenge of the stranger. This is clear from the epigraph by Alfred North Whitehead: "The clash of doctrines is not a disaster, it is an opportunity." Such an opportunity may not always look like one to the exclusive group that is suspicious of and challenged by the person who has not belonged to it from the beginning. But it is the case.

Noting the example of the Hindu social system, which rests on the hierarchy and also the mutual repulsion of the castes, Simmel noted "a certain amount of discord, inner divergence and outer controversy is organically tied up with the very elements that ultimately hold the group together." In other words, conflict with the other, in our case the religious stranger, is a group-binding element. It is there and then tempting to demonize that "other," the member of a different caste or religion.

We interrupt Coser on Simmel here to introduce a reinforcing theme from the American longshoreman-philosopher Eric Hoffer, as he wrote on hatred among groups: "[Heinrich] Heine suggests that what Christian love cannot do is effected by a common hatred. Mass movements can rise and spread without belief in a God, but never without belief in a devil."[9] When the devil is vivid, tangible, and near, hatred grows most, as in the German action against Jews on *their* "homeland."

Hoffer reported on a Japanese mission that came to Berlin in 1932 to study the appeal of National Socialism. The visitor marveled: "It is magnificent. I wish we could have something like it in Japan, only we can't, because we haven't got any Jews." Hoffer: "Common hatred unites the most heterogeneous elements." Societies marked by some kinds of diversity find themselves united if they can target

29

and hate a common foe. The diverse sets of Americans who united to sing, even to shout, *God Bless America*, after September 2001, were united by their awareness of the threat of a distant, elusive, stealthy, but still tangible foe, al-Qaeda, and subsequently for many Americans, "*the* Muslim." Some enjoined citizens to hate the enemy and many mass communicators bannered images of the enemy that made him even more hateful.

Simmel also found some more positive potential in the presence of the stranger. But first he concentrated on how perception of the stranger enhanced the vitality of the perceiving group. Often, opposition is the only means a people may have to express rebellion against "tyranny, arbitrariness, moodiness, tactlessness," and the like. "Our opposition makes us feel that we are not completely victims of the circumstances," he noted, and "this gives us inner satisfaction."

As an example: young Algerian men, heirs of revolutionaries against colonial France and people, resented the corrupt, military, repressive, only nominally Muslim leadership in their nation. So they joined militant Muslim groups and also vented hostility, in virtually hopeless social circumstances, against Western ambassadors, traders, missionaries, and mass communicators. They invented a common devil and found some inner satisfaction where they could not solve their problems.

What was it that turned that congenial if partly mysterious Christian neighbor of Muslims, Muslim neighbor of Christians, or Jewish neighbor of both into first an object of suspicion and then a subject of hatred? Simmel pointed out that people do not always enter a war because of hatred of the other; war is instead the agent of hatred. "It is *expedient* to hate the adversary with whom one fights, just as it is expedient to love a person whom one is tied to." It is expedient for the suicide bomber to hate the Jews, the Western victim of al-Qaeda to hate Osama bin Laden − something not hard to do − or the Israeli to hate the Palestinian as a Muslim, even if he happens to be a Christian Palestinian![10]

Still, the hostility is most intense when it is the neighbor who is the stranger. Coser quotes anthropologist Bronislaw Malinowski:

"Aggression like charity begins at home," a theme on which we touched when discussing the stranger under roof.[11] This feature also helps account for intra-denominational or intra-sectarian conflict. In the United States, Baptists do not fight Methodists: they fight Baptists. Catholics do not fight Protestants: they fight Catholics. In all these cases, estrangement among parties that once were united can provoke hatred at least as intense as that found between belongers and newcoming strangers.

Another insight by Simmel illumines the way groups that are suspicious, accusing, conflicting, and eventually hating, characteristically resist appeals for ceasefires and mutual forbearance. Around the world through much of the twentieth century, some religious people across the boundaries among faiths had set out to minimize religious hostilities, to promote engagement, and to work for the issuing of a form of concord, and the possibility of then bearing with the other. Around the world through the same century, we also noted the simultaneous rise of resistant groups, reinforced by their hatred not only of the stranger but also of the mediator who would work to bring about some measure of concord among enemies. We have met these resisters, as they are often called fundamentalist. In the United States, some evangelists during the crisis after terrorism struck the country with a wide rhetorical swing and declared Islam as such evil, wicked, and even demonic. In their eyes and those of their followers, efforts by anyone to foster understanding or harmony among the groups looked like a threat to national cohesion, and in their eyes such a person or movement was subversive.

Simmel had something to offer here, too. "Groups and especially minorities, which live in conflict and persecution, often reject approaches or tolerance from the other side. The closed nature of their opposition without which they cannot fight on would be blurred." Now, one may ask just how members of middle-class American evangelizing groups are suffering persecution. Two answers: first, some of the missionaries, regarded as their representatives, entered closed Muslim societies and offended leaders and people alike. Arrested and imprisoned, they spread the word and their imprisoners quickly became objects of hatred. Second, since all groups can point to some or other outside agent who demeans or inconveniences them, stories of such in this case get exaggerated and headlined; the more evil they can be seen to be, the more support will grow for militant agencies that oppose them.

In societies where those who had once been persecuted or where long-demeaned religious minorities have finally acquired power, as many Muslims and Christians in the poor world have done, their leaders will still find it profitable to point to and even exaggerate harassments and call them persecutions. Simmel, again: "A group's complete victory over its enemies is thus not always fortunate." This is so because "victory lowers the energy which guarantees the unity of the group; and the dissolving forces, which are always at work, gain hold." His counsel would be: "see to it that there be some enemies in order for the unity of the members to remain effective and for the group to remain conscious of this unity as its vital mission."

While Simmel spoke of the contrast between unity and antagonism among groups that were pursuing an identical aim in science, applying his vision to religious conflict illumines reasons why such conflict is most bitter. The neighbors, whether living down the block or as fellow citizens, can be made an object and hated if those who have belonged from the beginning can ground their suspicion and hatred in a particular ideology. Thus, Simmel noted:

> The parties' consciousness of being mere representatives of supra-individual claims, of fighting not for themselves but only for a cause, can give the conflict radicalism and mercilessness which find their analogy in the general behavior of certain very selfless and very idealistically inclined persons.[12]

Such conflict involves the whole personality, but victory will belong to the cause; so, Simmel observed, conflict "has a noble character." This assessment characterizes everything from the Protestant or Catholic fighting not only for local issues in Northern Ireland but for Protestant truth or Catholicism as a whole. Palestinian Muslims fortify themselves for suicide missions by reference to prayer in the mosque and to the will of Allah. When some Protestant and Catholic women in Northern Ireland together won the Nobel prize some years ago for their efforts to reduce hostility and move toward concord, they became objects of hate for many militants who belonged to their two separate and hostile communions. When an Israeli or a Palestinian leader moves to reduce tension, thus leading to some minimization of perceived enemy threats, he is hated and may well be assassinated by a fellow Israeli or a fellow Palestinian, who sees their victim as a stranger to the noble cause.

An apparently perplexing feature in the conflict of religious belongers versus strangers has to do with the fact that some leaders endeavor to cast their visual net as widely as possible, to encompass as many kinds of "the enemy" as possible. Then they give the enemy a common name and eliminate degrees of difference among them. Whoever had any trace of Jewish blood was anathema to the Nazis. There were not good Jews and bad Jews, concessive Jews and militant Jews, strongly German Jews and Bolshevik-minded Jews: only Jews. To militant American evangelizers, a Muslim is a Muslim. Each of Islam's attendants falls equally under the judgment of God and is doomed to hell as an agent of deception and mischief. Any one among them is seen as simply part of Islamdom, a civilization with which as a whole Christian civilization as a whole, they think, must contend.

Simmel noted in this case that "in view of the incomparable utility of unified organization for purposes of fight, one would suppose every party to be extremely interested in the opposed party's lack of unity." But there are contrary cases, he noted: in the situation of conflict, the party may "prefer that the opponent, too, take on [the form of unity]." Simmel illustrated this by showing how in many struggles the diversities of labor and the varieties of management get reduced to the singular: Labor-united versus Management-united. Strategically, this distinction should make little sense, since a divided enemy is both easier to conquer and, more positively, because there are more openings for concord, should it be sought. In such cases it usually is not sought.

It would be a mistake to suggest that those who "belong from the beginning" were themselves united from the beginning. Simmel observed how conflict gives rise to coalitions and then to associations. The National Conference of Christians and Jews in the United States was supported by people who observed the terror of Christian actions against Jews in Germany in the 1930s, or the folly of Catholic versus Protestant tensions in America when the resources of the two were needed in union against Soviet communism. Conflict, Simmel observed, may bring together persons and groups which have otherwise nothing to do with each other.

The Christian ecumenical movement drew strength from such association, just as internationally Christian, Jewish, and other religious groups formed themselves over against the atheism of communism or the secular humanism of some forces in the West. American Catholics and Evangelicals, long at odds with each other ("The pope is the Anti-Christ!"), suddenly formed associations to fight against abortionists, putting aside what in doctrine and practice both had long considered to be huge differences.[13]

It is also possible for a belonger to *become* a stranger, through conversion or the adoption of bewildering or antagonistic and thus alien behaviors and beliefs. Simmel and Coser shone spotlights on such persons, too. The treasonous person, the traitor to a nation, is always more despised than the enemy who never shared the privileges of having belonged. In the religious world, the heretic and the apostate are more mistrusted and hated than the heathen who never was spiritually anywhere near the group of belongers. "People who have many common features often do one another worse or 'worser' wrong than complete strangers do," wrote Simmel of people who became incomplete strangers but, in his eyes, still menaces. He noted how threatening to a religious "neighborhood," a denomination or sect or religious body, is the figure of the renegade, the apostate. With good reason.

Simmel spelled out the reason. The renegade breaks down the boundaries that protected the established group. The rabbis from the time of the Maccabees onward had to concern themselves with such threats. The peculiar power of the one who chooses to become a stranger resides in the fact that, as Simmel observed, having chosen to leave, he has had to become or be seen as a betrayer, never to be trusted again. He cannot go back. Simmel quoted philosopher Max Scheler on this point: the apostate or renegade, proving loyalty to his new community, must "engage in a continuous chain of acts of revenge on his spiritual past."[14]

The Muslim who converts "out" can face the death penalty in some Islamic cultures. The Jew who marries a Gentile and converts to Christianity can be ostracized and excluded from some Jewish communities. The ex-Catholic priest who had left the church before the changes wrought by the Second Vatican Council (1962–5) was a popular figure on the Protestant anti-Catholic circuit, because he was trusted to have inside knowledge and was ready to spill it to audiences that were already hostile to Catholicism. Discounting the fact that such an apostate might bring a distorting or blinding passion against what he left behind, non- and anti-Catholics back then celebrated his type. Obviously, he was more hated by Catholic belongers than were those who had never been Catholic, no matter how anti-Catholic the latter naturally were. Messianic Jews and groups like Jews for Jesus (Jews converted to "born again" Christianity who are seeking to make more such converts) are especially scorned by Jews who remained faithful to their own interpretation of the covenant.[15]

All these instances illustrate how much is at stake when faiths collide, when religion is at issue among belongers and strangers, in any number of circumstances. The most menacing is the world of *realpolitik*, where efficient surveillance and sophisticated weaponry are in the hands of the religious strangers on the level of the nations. Some of them met some of the problem by inventing and adapting to constitutional systems and historical practices in which they could remain a believer and a citizen at the same time.

35

3

When Faith Communities Conflict

The Stranger on the National Scene

While the presence of strangers in the home or the neighborhood can be disconcerting and disruptive, the modern nation is the site for most contention in our time. The nation as a modern liberal invention in post-Enlightenment times tended to be seen as legally profane (*pro + fanum*, "outside the sanctuary"). In other words, this secular creation was not necessarily hostile to religion, and faith communities have often thrived there. Where more than one of these was present, there was always the possibility of clashes among them, or between any and all of them and secular forces, including those of the nation itself. To appraise something of the contemporary context, the historical background in the United States can serve for illumination. This is the case because its Constitution was intentionally godless, but its drafters and the majority of citizens who succeeded them have been part of faith communities.

Article VI of the United States Constitution of 1787 explicitly ruled out religious tests for holders of office. This was intended to prevent any religion from claiming the right to belong in a privileged way. In the First Amendment to that Constitution, just as its drafters stated "Congress shall make no law . . . prohibiting the free exercise of religion," they wrote also that it "shall make no law respecting an establishment of religion." Courts and publics may interpret that phrase in endless variations, but in the formal legal sense the founders certainly intended to place the Congress and (as interpreted by the Supreme Court after the 1940s) also the states, beyond the reach of formal and established religious encouragements, strictures, and interpretations.

Some nations were more formally secular. France in 1905 passed laws ensuring strict secularity in the public realm. The Constitution of India pre-1947 took on a non-religious character and ensured religious freedom. In Turkey in 1918, Ataturk worked to extricate that nation from the official hold of Islam, and the nation declared itself to be legally non-religious.

Not many citizens were fooled, however, by these forms of dis-establishment, unless the laws supporting them were enforced by the military, as in the case of Turkey. Catholicism, though weakened as a church in aggressively secular France, remains a reminiscent presence, as is Islam in Turkey. The ruling parties in India – the BJP and the RSS – are hardline religious groups who build on the ethos of pre-947 Hindu India at the expense of Muslim India. Hindus and Muslims, in the carving up that produced the boundaries of modern India, are strangers to each other, and are in regular conflict.

Georg Simmel's way of combining the themes of shared space and cultural belonging over against the stranger, the alien, and the immigrant informs the situations just mentioned, but is also appropriate elsewhere. The citizenry of Britain, because it retains an established Church of England, might have been expected to be hostile to strangers beyond that church. However, the decline in population and the cooling of commitment along with the growth of other religious bodies has changed the way Britons feel about who belongs and who does not. They had to, given the numbers. While further declensions have since occurred, by 1990 the Church of England attracted only 37 percent of the people, while Roman Catholics represented 11 percent. Active church membership declined by one half, from 22 percent to 11 percent between 1970 and 1990, and was still dropping in 2000. Only 55 percent of the British thought of themselves as religious persons.

Religion as such therefore was not always at the base of inter-group hostilities in Britain after a million Muslims arrived in recent decades, to make up 2 percent of the population. By 1990 there were also 500,000 Sikhs and 300,000 Jews. Only Anglicans and Roman Catholics drew more active participants than did the newcoming Muslims. Often described as among the least religious of the industrialized nations, Britain found that its established church was of little help in arresting the decline of religious participation and belief. The religions of strangers prospered at its expense.

Whereas in Britain there had been perhaps 70,000 South Asians in the middle of the twentieth century, more than 2 million lived there at the century's end. In earlier times most of them had been temporary, poor, and exploited people. Yet out of that culture there emerged a small number of notables, among them Krishna Menon, a friend of Jawaharlal Nehru and an agent for producing better circumstances for South Asians in Britain. A literary figure who helped found Penguin Books, he was politically best known as Britain's abrasive representative at the United Nations. But such emergences as Menon's were still few. The careers of these strangers among the British belongers demonstrate how difficult it has been for such to move into citizenship and respectability.[1]

In Germany, with its long history of religious conflict but also of a once-strong establishment of Roman Catholic and Evangelical (Lutheran and Reformed) churches, ethnic homogeneity held fairly well. In 1990, 93 percent of the people were ethnically German. Most of the rest were *Gastarbeiter*, "guest-worker" strangers mainly from Turkey and the former Yugoslavia. Catholic and Evangelical church rolls then each numbered over one third of the population, while 3 percent were Muslims. After the Holocaust few Jews survived or returned, and their population remains at less than 1 percent.[2]

Further to set the stage for comparison of polities and strangers, we observe the Netherlands, where Dutch Reformed churches had been established and privileged for centuries. By the 1990s, during a time of drastic decline in church participation, Catholics and Protestants each drew nominal attachment from about 4.5 million people in a population of about 15 million. Home to international populations for some time, it now numbers 600,000 Muslims, most of them from Turkey and Morocco, while there were about 80,000 each of Hindus and Buddhists living in this constitutional monarchy.[3]

A journalist's report in 2002 described the situation when long-time inhabitants of the Netherlands were having difficulty trying to relate to immigrants. According to Rod Dreher, Pim Fortuyn (a libertarian politician murdered in May of that year) had illustrated how "the secular West was in the midst of a clash of civilizations with intolerant Islam." Fortuyn's anti-immigration program explicitly opposed multiculturalism, in a nation that had pioneered in fostering a polity of pluralism. The citizens called this *Verzuiling*, which meant that Catholics, Protestants, and secularists had organized life around their own "pillars" and formed distinct cultures.

During and after the 1960s the Netherlands changed more drastically than any other Western nation, some say, from a nation that exemplified a conservative Christian ethos to one that became a secular, materialist, hedonist culture. In thirty years, weekly church attendance went down from 60 percent to around 8–13 percent. Dreher quoted an American expert, Hope College professor James Kennedy: "A number of Dutch religious and secular leaders concluded there wasn't a lot to be done to resist. One thing the Dutch political culture does well, maybe too well, is to accommodate itself to new moods in society." That adaptive character, however, did not prepare the citizens to cope with some of the new immigrants, strangers to the Dutch and the secular Western ethos alike. The government subsidizes religious schools. One third of the Muslim schools are also funded by Muslims who lean toward extremism, and one-fifth of them receive funds from explicitly radical Islamic groups. How largely secular and genially tolerant Netherlanders will continue to accommodate themselves to such neighbors will command attention for years to come.[4]

Another case study could be Australia, which bears at least as many marks of religious decline as do most European nations. In 1991 there were a few more Catholics than Anglicans (4.6 million to 4 million), plus a substantial Uniting Church and other Protestants. But among these Christians were also 1.3 million Muslims, 150,000 Buddhists, and 75,000 Jews.[5] In 1999 Australia included the largest percentage of immigrants in the population of any nation; about one-fourth of the Australian population was "foreign." Next in line were Canada, Sweden, the United States, the Netherlands, and Austria. Six Western nations in all counted more than 10 percent of their populations as foreign or, in a news magazine's tally, they made up "the company of strangers." The top three of these, their population base having been built on immigration, tended to be more ready to welcome more strangers. Japan, where only 1 or 2 percent were listed as foreign, was least familiar with the stranger, and seen to be more suspicious and less welcoming than others. The same magazine pointed to the special problems religion brings when immigrants arrive in formerly more homogeneous societies:

> Some of the children of Germany's Turks, Britain's Pakistanis, and France's North Africa seem more attracted to fundamentalism than their parents are. If Muslims take their religions seriously, is that deplorable or admirable? If Islam constrains women and attacks homosexuality, what are the boundaries to freedom of speech and religion? Even societies that feel at ease with change will find such questions hard.[6]

The United States' Constitutional Background

The United States also has recently seen the regeneration of a phenomenon called, variously, "civil religion," "public religion," "the civic faith," or "the religion of the Republic." Such religion comes furnished with quasi-religious symbols, encourages religious ceremonies, stamps "In God We Trust" on its coins and currency, and hears eruptions of songs such as "God Bless America" at public gatherings, especially in times of national uncertainty.

The United States case demands close study, since that nation has been seen as most pluralistic and has a record of receiving immigrants through its entire life. Its case does differ from that of nations where the population was demonstrably more homogeneous. The United States has seen a progression through more than three centuries of interactions between belongers and strangers and among strangers who came to make the nation their new home. In most cases, religion was an agent that helped produce situations of exclusivity and rejection among the subcommunities, be they Catholic, Jewish, and many sorts of Protestant, including African American, Latter-day Saint, and scores more.

The mainly English-speaking Protestant Europeans who arrived after 1607 as the strangers who came to stay rapidly established themselves, at least in their own eyes, as owners of the space. The native people who often at first had welcomed them regarded them like Simmel's stranger, as "the wanderer who comes today and goes tomorrow." In Massachusetts Bay, Virginia, and elsewhere the Native-American Indians were often hospitable and generous in sharing food, goods, and know-how that enabled the first settlers to survive. But when the natives gradually came to see that the settler was "the person who comes today and stays tomorrow" and who came in great numbers with guns and ships, some Indians attacked, as they did on Good Friday in 1622 at Henrico in Virginia. Wars followed there and elsewhere in the colonies.

From the beginning, diseases imported from Europe, plagues against which the Indians had no immunity, unbelievably murderous policies, the preemption of land, and the reservating and the killing of Indians all devastated the prior population. Many of the anti-Indian moves occurred with religious justifications. Whatever the terms used to define the land, whether God's New Israel, Zion, the Lord's vineyard, God's city set upon a hill, or still others, it was clear that the newcomer had taken over the continental neighborhood in the name of God. Later, as the nation was being formed, when it came to the

41

Native Americans, who should have been the belongers, exclusivity ruled. The United States Constitution officially regarded the native people as a foreign power, to be dealt with as such.

Two founders as belongers

Before long the white newcomers took over so decisively that a Simmel could well have made a case study of belongers by citing some of the national founders. The classic statement of belonging in a landscape was written by John Jay in the second *Federalist* paper, published in 1787 at a time when Jay, James Madison, and Alexander Hamilton were selling the Constitution to the colonies that were becoming states.

Jay was an ardent nationalist. His time spent in Europe led him to reject what we are calling tribalism among white people, largely homogenizing them, and to come to love the American landscape with its civil possibilities. A devoutly religious man who did not shun the pleasures of the world, Jay was vain, elitist, and in love with property and the power that went with it. "Those who own the country ought to govern it."[7]

He devoted himself little to the questions of human rights, which were so prominent in the political discourse of the day, but was almost obsessively devoted to the task of nation building. He argued that the colonies, though now connected only in weak Confederation, *were* a nation and therefore needed a regime. He was answering the pseudonymous Brutus and Cato [for the record, probably Richard Henry Lee and George Clinton], who were contending that Americans were too dissimilar to form a Federal Union at all. Americans to them looked so diverse that citizens must remain content with more local governmental patterns, in which cases more homogeneous populations held sway.

Since we are making John Jay an exemplar of Georg Simmel's notes about *place* and *belonging*, let me enlarge a bit and observe him stressing that the string of colonies along the Atlantic Coast were not "composed of detached and distant territories, but that one connected, fertile, wide spreading country was the portion of our western sons of liberty." *Connected* was his key. But nationhood also meant the need for a people who had much in common, so he stated his case beginning with observations about ethnicity. Jay himself, who had no English blood, being five-eighths Dutch and three-eighths French, was writing in a time when some of his own work had to be translated into German for the German speakers of the nation. He conveniently overlooked such exceptions. Like so many leaders, he personally had experienced some overcoming of ethnic, national, and linguistic heritages and had become assimilated into the Anglo world. Simmel might have rubbed his hands together in glee to see this part of his theory confirmed: that fighting a common enemy has a group binding effect. Here is Jay:

> Providence has been pleased to give this one connected country to one united people – a people descended from the same ancestors, speaking the same language, *professing the same religion*, attached to the same principles of government, very similar in their manners and customs, and who, by their joint counsels, arms, and efforts, fighting side by side throughout a long and bloody war, have nobly established general liberty and independence.
>
> This country and this people seem to have been made for each other, and it appears as if it was the design of Providence, that an inheritance so proper and convenient for a band of brethren, united to each other by the strongest ties, should never be split into a number of unsocial, jealous, or alien sovereignties.
>
> Similar sentiments have hitherto prevailed among all orders and denominations of men among us. To all general purposes we have uniformly been one people; each individual citizen everywhere enjoying the same national rights, privileges, and protection. As a nation we have made peace and war; as a nation we have vanquished our common enemies; as a nation we have formed alliances.[8]

What Jay penned was effective; it played its part in shaping a nation of belongers. One analyst of the *Federalist* papers says that nationalist thought had not been well developed by 1787: "Jay's

43

statement is not only strong, but also quite advanced. When it appeared, it was probably the most lucid description of a nation that had ever been penned."[9]

Jay was not to have his way in respect to future unfoldings of American life. Indeed, he had not had his way already by the time he was writing. Note his language in those three short paragraphs. He was selling the Constitution so that "unsocial, jealous, or alien sovereignties" – the England it had just fought off, or the potential nations that the colonies might become – would not disrupt the emerging nation. We need not make too large a point of it that about half of the citizenry, meaning women, was only an implied population in his language. They had no voting rights. It was also clear that many other groups on the scene, in Simmel's phrase, had not "belonged to it from the beginning." And now they had to be regarded as "alien," which meant as foreign as England had now become in the eyes of nativists like Jay.

His language was appropriate to those he numbered as belongers to "one nation." Five times he referred to the citizens of the colonies with the same word, "same," three times with "one," two times with "similar," just as he spoke of them being "side by side," "united," and "uniform[ly]" facing "common" enemies and forming "alliances."

As was the case with the Constitution, Jay's writing did not include or imply that the Native Americans who shared the space, were being driven from it, were dying off, or being killed, belonged. Ironically, they had by now instead come to be seen as the strangers and foreigners. Similarly, Jay did not mention the African Americans who had arrived as strangers and aliens against their will. Jews, Catholics, "infidels," and even other kinds of Protestants who had flooded into Pennsylvania and others of the middle and southern colonies did not meet his criteria for full belonging, as he instinctively but eloquently expressed them. They were Lutheran, Reformed, and Anabaptists (Mennonite, Brethren, and the like) who did not share what Jay called the same ancestors, language, principles of government, manners, and customs. He was correct only in the broadest sense when he argued that these all were of the "same religion," Protestant Christianity. But the cultural gulfs among them at that time were huge, as were the religious points of difference.

We have as witness for that observation another national founder, at least as much an heir of the Enlightenment as Jay had been: Benjamin Franklin. When Germans migrated into Philadelphia, this tolerant citizen-leader became as uneasy with them as he was with blacks and Catholics: "This will in a few years become a German colony." He went on in this writing of 1751 to say that evidently "instead of learning our language, we must learn theirs or live as in a foreign country." He led off with "Why should the Palatine boors [*bauerntopels* – "blockheads"] be suffered to swarm into our settlements, and by herding together establish their language and manners to the execution of ours?" He could not have been more pointed: "Why should Pennsylvania, founded by the English, become a colony of *aliens*, who will shortly be so numerous as to Germanize us instead of our Anglifying them, and will never adopt our language or customs, any more than they can acquire our complexion?"[10] Franklin may have grown more tolerant of diversity by 1787, but he reflected the cultural context of many elites in the Anglo linguistic and religious communities.

From the stranger who was Native and had no rights and the African American, usually a slave, who had none, we turn to the strangers called immigrants who came in greater numbers after the forming of the nation. They suffered more from ethos than restrictive laws, from snubs and harassments or economic discrimination by earlier-arriving citizens than from legislators. Some were Jews, more were Catholics, who did not share Jay's "same [Protestant] religion" or manners. While rejection of Jews, always few in number until the 1880s, was not always connected with religious persecution, most Jews definitely were considered strangers in much of national life. Catholics, who shared the Christian faith to which Jay pointed, were considered strangers sufficiently to inspire what came to be known as Nativism. Nativists, as their name implied, averred that they had belonged "from the beginning" in the American space. They engaged for a long period in a Protestant Crusade against the Catholics as infidels in their relation to American civil-religious values.

For a long time the advocates of presumed homogeneity in the host culture had much of their own way. Immigration laws had been designed to cut down the numbers and to ensure the proper ethnic and religious stock among immigrants. President Franklin D. Roosevelt, who shared some Dutch ancestry with John Jay, was thoroughly at home with and was typed by Anglo-religious (Anglicanism = Episcopal) membership, and also brought credentials of the historic elites. In 1938 he reminded the Daughters of the American Revolution of the fact that they and all other Americans were "immigrants." The DAR was a group whose *raison d'être* was to ensure the protected and elite status of those whose husbands would have satisfied Jay with their ancestry, customs, manners, and descent from those who had fought a common war against an enemy. They considered that they were here "from the beginning," unlike most Jews, Irish, Italians, and the like. Roosevelt's opening words were true but jarring: "Fellow immigrants . . ."

Liberal societies and the terms of belonging

However anticipated in the founding, in the course of time in all the nations mentioned, including the United States, what developed was a form of liberal society. This is a creation that warrants spelling out and observation, so determinative is it for understanding what happens and what can happen when faiths collide. An economical definition which will serve well here is offered by Robert Booth Fowler:

> By *liberalism* . . . I mean . . . (1) a commitment to skeptical reason, an affirmation of pragmatic intelligence, and an uneasiness about both abstract philosophical thinking and non-rational modes of know-ledge; (2) enthusiasm in principle (and increasingly in practice) for tolerance not only in political terms but more obviously in terms of lifestyle and social norms; (3) affirmation of the central importance of the individual and individual freedom.[11]

The great theorists of liberal society in the West – John Locke, John Stuart Mill, and John Dewey – in one important catalogue, may have had respect for aspects of religion, though it must be said, there was a declining respect by the time of Dewey. He wanted to replace the inherited religions with what he called *A Common Faith*.[12] Jeff Spinner-Halev, who examined these figures, noted how they hypothesized or took for granted that as societies and religion progressed, there would be ever less religion, ever less intense faith, and ever more wan witness to an ever more relaxed deity. After Locke, he wrote, these thinkers and their contemporaries in the various generations "thought that over time people would lose their attachments to revealed religion and would embrace a religion that centered around humanity, not God."[13] Spinner-Halev turned report into safe prophecy: "The liberal project to turn people toward more liberal religions will not be completely – or even close to completely – successful any time soon." He urged that liberals should argue with conservatives, but never with the expectation that the enclave groups would soon fade. He offered three principles that can become part of this manifesto:

> Allowing people to choose the religious conservative life within the confines of citizenship leads me to develop three principles. The first is *non-interference*. A cultural community that meets certain minimal conditions can exist without interference from the liberal state. The second is *inclusion*. I argue that the liberal state should try to include religious conservatives in its institutions and in public debate when religious conservatives want to do so, and when doing so does not undercut citizenship. The third principle is *exclusion*: people should be able to exclude others from their institutions, as long as doing so does not harm citizenship.

We may have reason to question the word "allowing:" who is the "allowing" group and who makes up the cast of monitors? Yet Spinner-Halev was chiefly addressing liberals who do not find any of the three easy to follow when dealing with conservatives, who are intellectual strangers to them. In fact, he chided his fellow liberals for their tone-deafness to religious voices and their frequent inconsistencies. He contended that, ironically, "many recent arguments favor diversity but do little to ease the tensions between liberal and conservative religions and may even increase them." In his observation but our terms, they become two more tribes, each thinking of itself as the original belongers and the other as strangers in liberal societies which house them both.[14]

Spinner-Halev is typical of a company of those who judge liberal society from within, critics who bemoan the intolerance directed by many against the religiously intolerant, or against the religious in any mode. These are people who suffer from silence, neglect, expressions of disdain, or automatic exclusion from the counsels of a liberal society. Not only does he want religion restored as an object of discussion, and not only do he and others like him not argue grudgingly. They go on, or at least here he goes on, to advertise the civic purposes that religious groups can and often do pursue. In an important passage he compares religious to other mediating institutions, using the language of communities called churches:

> *Some* church activity does support liberal virtues. Civic skills learned in the workplace are deeply stratified by class, race, and gender; in non-political voluntary associations they are stratified by class and race. In churches, however, participation is not stratified: "The domain of equal access of opportunities to learn civic skills is in the church." [He is quoting Sidney Verba, Kay Lehman Schlozman, and Henry E. Brady, students of voluntarism.] Participation here means not mere attendance. It means planning meetings, attending meetings where decisions are made, writing letters, and making a speech or presentation.[15]

Spinner-Halev does admit that different religious bodies and congregations, whether on the religious and political left or right, are not equal in their participation in liberal societies. Yet he has helped point to what events and trends in society have confirmed: that religion can no longer be overlooked in public life and that argument about religion has great civic implications. The more the role of religion gets acknowledged, the more urgent is a revisitation of its roots. These have much to say about the relation of belongers to strangers. In the most familiar forms in the West, as a foundation for Judaism and Christianity, this means dealing with the Bible, which the majority of religious factions in the United States convoke as authoritative and inspirational.

The biblical background for dealing with the stranger

The issue of the stranger antedates by far the sophisticated essay by Simmel or the arguments of inventors of liberal societies, including the American founders. In the latter case, while they drew on many Greek and Roman classical sources, they were also leaders in colonies where Protestant Christian settlers made much of the Bible. From the first Pilgrim and Puritan writings in New England after 1620 and 1630, the prototype, model, paradigm, template, and exemplum for the colonies was ancient Israel.

The New Testament offered little counsel as to how to govern a state, so the pious and dedicated founders resorted to the Hebrew scriptures, and especially to what they called Mosaic Law and modern scholars see condensed in the Deuteronomic Code. I will draw on Harold V. Bennett's *Injustice Made Legal* for much of the following discussion of that Deuteronomic Law. In the contexts surrounding such law, it was clear that the relation of the belongers and the strangers posed an urgent issue for the nomadic and newly conquering people who were establishing their government and, by analogy, their nation in the Northern Kingdom. A series of laws that included reference to the stranger took shape in that time and place, as detailed in the biblical book of Deuteronomy 14:22–29; 16:9–12, 13–15; 24:17–18, 19–22, and 26:12–15.

The purpose in citing also a number of scholars with whom Bennett argues in efforts to establish who all were the strangers is to show how dazzlingly complex was that world which so many moderns picture as having been simple. Then, as now, the question of exactly who is the stranger and what being a stranger means is not easy to answer. This means that then, as now, a number of strategies for dealing with the stranger were necessary.

In the cast of characters, first is one of the tribes, the Levites, who were set aside as priests. They were included as semi-outsiders in these laws, "because they have no allotment or inheritance with you" (14:29 NRSV). The real outsiders in their place, however, were strangers, who are referred to as "resident aliens." They needed special treatment, along with orphans and widows. Other translations of the Bible also have the stranger being the "alien" (NAB) or "foreigner" (NJB). In any case, the setting places this person "in your towns" (NRSV), "in your settlements" (REB), and "your community" (NAB and NJB), the "your" meaning the people of Israel, who considered that they were the belongers in each case. Compare these to newly arrived immigrants in the Netherlands or Britain, Australia or Germany.

The point is this: strangers had to be reckoned with because they were close at hand, where the townspeople, the settled settlers, and the community were in place and where these belongers shared much by way of outlook. As for their analogue to modern religions of nationalism or civil religions, in cultic observances (16:11–12) the same trio of strangers in the form of aliens or foreigners, along with orphans and widows, were to be included at the times when the belongers would "rejoice before the Lord [their] God." The ritual leaders were to use the occasion to help the people remember their own stranger status as slaves in Egypt. In 24:17–28 we read that the Israelites were not to deprive the same trio, including the stranger, "the resident alien," and "the foreigner," of justice. They were to leave a residue of sheaves in the field, olives on the tree, or grapes on the vine for such to pick up, again, always remembering that Israel had been strangers enslaved in Egypt. It would be easy to find analogies here to social policies with which long-established citizens are to regard the impoverished and displaced new arrivals.

Who were these strangers, and why did they carry so much importance that they had to be included in the Deuteronomic Code? Harold V. Bennett surveys and cites the extensive literature of argument over who was the stranger, the *gēr* in biblical communities. To some biblical scholars they were persons "who lived permanently in a tribal area where [they] had no consanguine relations, no blood kin, and thus [were] bereft of socioeconomic and legal protection." In the eyes of another scholar, they "can only be the conquered, not wholly but nearly assimilated early population."

The sociologist contemporary of Simmel, Max Weber, argued the *gēr* was of foreign stock from elsewhere in the biblical community, but not a full member of the host community. Normally he was landless, probably someone therefore who had to find a patron among the landed to survive. Another scholar found the stranger to be a free person, who did not have the "full civic rights" that children of Israel had. Still another looked to the Southern Kingdom and assumed that the stranger was a fugitive from the Northern.

Bennett presents the arguments of Christiana van Houten, Christoph Bultmann, and Frank A. Spina on who was the stranger. He agrees most with Spina, who stressed the immigrant status of the stranger. Such a person may have arrived for any number of reasons, all of them similar to the occasions for migration and settlement today: "famine, war, the failure to incite revolution or to secure pasturage or the seeker of asylum." So this "immigrant," to employ a better term than "resident alien," bore and reflected socioeconomic problems brought along to Israel. Spina had written: "It is my contention that *gēr* should be translated by a word that underscores not simply the outsider status in the adopted social setting, but in addition those factors and conditions related to the emigration in the first place."

Christiana van Houten found the stranger to be "a non-Israelite who lived among the Israelites," perhaps an Edomite, a Moabite, or an Ammonite. Christoph Bultmann made an important point: the *gēr* was not a stranger in Israel, and was never described as such, but "a stranger in a local milieu . . . a stranger in relation to an individual respective village of his residence." To continue our comparisons: in the legal structure of modern liberal societies, a federal government may make provision for the rights of the immigrant, but that newcomer still may be shunned by those who consider themselves as belongers who can set the terms for life in their locales.

Picture in our time a member of the Nation of Islam whose firm transfers him from a thick cluster of such Muslims in Detroit to a Baptist community in Alabama. Or a Lubavitscher Jew who moves from New York to Postville, Iowa, to work for relatives there who manage a plant in the chicken industry. Neither comes from a foreign land to a new country, but from another place within the same country to a locale where his presence causes suspicion and disruption. He simply represents internal migration in a situation where unlike comes to meet like. While our two examples were middle class, in Bultmann's view, and in that of most of the other scholars as well, the internal migrant occupied a lower socioeconomic position, one that was disturbing to the previously present belongers, as Mexican migratory workers are in many United States communities today.

Bennett's summary of biblical settings demonstrates their relevance to the United States of 1787 as well as in the new millennium:

> The attitude of the *gēr* toward the culture of the mainstream is the issue that delimited this type of individual in the biblical communities. That is to say, cultural distance, or what G. Simmel describes as "the absence of commonness," should be the distinguishing feature of the *gēr* in the DC [Deuteronomic Code]. Simmel argues that the *other* in human societies does not seek to assimilate into the mainstream, and that he/she is likely to meander and not to have a specified or conclusively determined status in the host community.[16]

Bennett revisits what we have stressed about the stranger in the classic writing by Simmel: "that he has not belonged to [the host community] from the beginning, that he imports qualities into it, which do not and cannot stem from the group itself." While Bennett stressed socioeconomic features, near the end of his book he also deals with the cultic, or with what we might call the religious dimension. It happens that there was internal conflict in Canaan and now Israel as well. The children of Israel were in contention with each other and their religious competitors. Bennett refers to the belongers in "the Yahweh-Alone Cult," described in the prophet stories of Elijah and Elisha in 1 and 2 Kings. As a monotheistic group this exclusive cult was in contention with various henotheisms. The Yahweh-Alone people were "absolutist" and "intolerant," as the Elijah stories show (1 Kings 17–19; 2 Kings 1–8:15 and 10).[17]

Another comment by Bennett, who cites psychologist Gordon Allport, also will inform some of our inquiries about the ambiguous, paradoxical, and contradictory potential in religion when it serves the belongers as hosts when they deal with the strangers. As the Yahweh-Alone group fought the worshipers of Baalim:

> The hostilities between these camps illustrate the belief that the quest to advance one's religious program invites brutality, bigotry, and the systematic destruction of human beings; all in the name of piety. Regarding the relationship of religiousness to humanization, Allport writes: "The role of religion is paradoxical. It makes prejudice, and it unmakes prejudice. While the creeds of the great religions are universalistic, stressing brotherhood, the practice of these creeds is frequently divisive and brutal. The sublimity of religious ideals is offset by the horrors of persecution in the name of the same ideal." [18]

In Bennett's view, the Yahweh-Alone group drafted the Deuteronomic Code, generous sounding though it be, to protect their own interests. He finds the Code to be protective of the elites, the cultic leaders, while the peasants had to carry the onus for supporting the administration group. Thus they became outraged that the elite was siphoning off their meager yield. Some of the nice-sounding language about sharing the cultic observances with the stranger were written to enforce the details of such observances, thus granting more power to the drafting elite: "the self-interest of priests and prophets shaped these laws." In sum, another paradox is here: the Code looks liberal and generous, but it was written partly to legitimate and reinforce socioeconomic policies that in the end worked against the stranger. Such activity is not unknown among elites in modern liberal societies.

Some of Bennett's reasoning at the end is speculative. But his final point need not be established by clear evidence for our purposes: it simply alerts us to observe the host cultures of belongers – be they in the world of Elijah or John Jay or our contemporaries – with fresh eyes.[19]

After observing, it is in place to see how these texts situate the stranger, pointing as they do both to obligations by hosts and challenges posed by the *gēr*. American colonists and nation builders as exclusivists knew what they were doing when they chose to see their own story against the backdrop of ancient Israel and what they found in *their* Great Code, the Hebrew Bible. Contemporaries who legislate for immigrants and agencies who deal with them, including religious organizations, wrestle still with distinctions as old as the Deuteronomic Code. Not all of them are as generous in spirit as were these lawgivers long ago.

Cultural Evolution and the Privilege of the Belongers

The Yahweh-Alone cultic leadership, like the elites who did the drafting of documents for the American Revolutionaries and Constitution and established elites in most nations, exploited their situations of power, sometimes for human good but often for inflicting the bad. To understand why for so long they prevailed over all comers I turn, as I have often through the years, to a speculative anthropological theory posed by a team of cultural evolutionists in 1960. It is not necessary to buy their theory as a "law," and I do not; to me it is a creative observation. David Kaplan posed it as the "Law of Cultural Dominance":

> That cultural system which more effectively exploits the energy resources of a given environment will tend to spread in that

environment at the expense of less effective systems . . . Put another way, the law states that a cultural system will tend to be found precisely in those environments in which it yields a higher energy return per unit of human labor than any alternative system available.[20]

This Law-turned-Observation helps explain the advantages of the Yahweh-Alone leadership in ancient Israel and the heirs of the privileged "homogeneous" people described by John Jay in the nation he saw and whose development he foresaw. They were on the scene longer than later comers; they had guns to remove the Indians and chains to enslave the blacks. So they had comparatively free rein to "exploit the energy resources," both natural and human, that Jay so eloquently described. The strangers in the form of the immigrants might upset all that, especially if they brought other value systems, manners, "qualities," and religions than those already dominant among the citizens who had been there for a long time.

The reservations to which Indians were removed were in regions which offered few apparent energy resources. They were moved to the dry Great Plains. There the vanishing buffalo was an anticipation of what many whites hoped would be the vanishing Indian. Or they were restricted to places like the drier Southwest, a virtually resourceless desert. Simmel would have made much of the history of legal boundary-setting. Emancipated black slaves were segregated on southern farms as sharecroppers or crowded together in ranks of the socioeconomic lowest in the city. Someone other than they had access to the energy resources. By the mere fact of their presence, or with their interest as late comers in catching up with some use of the natural and human resources, segregated blacks were threats, as they fought for a place in the large but preempted space that Jay described and envisioned.

Through the years in the United States, often called a "nation of strangers," citizens and new immigrants have seen an unfolding of various strategies. More often than not they succeeded in helping form some version of Jay's "one nation," one whose emergence is always in process, always being tested. They knew that they did not

55

want to revert to the patterns of Holy War that their ancestors had seen in Europe from the time of the Crusades to the Thirty Years War and in countless intergroup conflicts. While in colonial times they might banish the strangers within (dissenters like Anne Hutchinson or Roger Williams), or kill a few (like Quaker Mary Dyer), they watched many later-arriving dissenting groups make their way and eventually belong. They disestablished the churches, legally removing the privilege of those who had belonged longest in the colonial environment. Grudgingly, yet eventually, they accepted millions of immigrants, strangers making their way in transforming their new home.

The truth in Malinowski's epigram, however, that "aggression like charity begins at home," was displayed in the greatest tragedy in the nation's life, in the most savage war in history fought to that point. The Civil War was a conflict that displayed the high price paid by two peoples for their estrangement. Most of the way between 1861 and 1865 those who fought it were precisely the heirs of those Jay had described. Most still were of English and certainly of European ancestry. Most spoke English. Most were Protestant Christian or at least Christian. They believed they were in the right in their interpretation of the "same principles of government." While new cultures were developing in the two regions called North and South, citizens in both places still shared what Simmel referred to as similarities in their manners and customs. Yet Southerners in the Confederate States of America saw Northerners as estranged, while Northerners defending the Union perceived Southerners as monstrous strangers. Nothing of any Deuteronomic Code ethic survived in those years.

After that central moment in American history, immigrants who did not fit Jay's description of belongers kept coming as strangers and gradually fought and found their way. In the new century, after forty years of severe immigration restriction, new legislation in 1965 opened the door more widely, and millions of newcomers arrived. Many belongers perceived Muslims, Sikhs, refugees from Southeast Asia, newcoming Africans, and many more as challenges. Though the record is mixed, the course was long, and legislative battles were intense, national law increasingly protected them.

Their challenge, and the challenge of their hosts, matched the situation of strangers' existence as described by Christopher Bultmann: their challenge was "in the local milieu," next door, down the street, or, as it turned out in the United States, within the Protestant churches that had once united against strangers but now saw fissures that left many of them estranged from each other. Since what happened there in the 1920s and after parallels worldwide movements, the incident and phenomenon demand attention in the present context.

The Stranger as Fundamentalist

No dialectic of the belonger and the stranger, no story of estrangement and divorce within inherited denominational patterns, has been more intense in recent decades than that between "everyone else" and the fundamentalist.

Fundamentalism is a term coined on the soil of American Protestantism and the term, in various translations – not all of them welcome in all cultures – has traveled internationally. The invention of the word, which cannot be found in dictionaries before the 1920s, and its rapid spread in usage, occurred because a new phenomenon was present.

Picture the development something like this: in the course of centuries most cultures with a religious dimension, which may mean all cultures where the religious impulse is not systematically suppressed, will take on a traditional character. That is, a population or a major religious group within a denomination, accumulates memories, engages in communal practices, and quite likely insists on some sort of codification of these. In other words, most people who are relatively content or unable to picture mobilizing discontent, become conservative. They unthinkingly act on the basis of strategies that have produced solutions in the past. The codes become orthodox,

57

and the ancient scripts, if there are such, are determined to be class-ical and normative.

Such a population of belongers, by habit or choice, gets challenged by some force or other. The challenge may come as a result of new national alignments, foreign trade, or signals produced by mass media of communication. The aggressive belongers put up their guard so as not to be contaminated. Then they turn their defensiveness into policies designed to confine the strangers ("the ghetto") or remove them, rarely by force in liberal societies, but through many kinds of restrictions. Just as often, however, they may make some adjustments and compromises which may satisfy the majority but leave some discontented and in dissent.

It is from this cohort of the population that fundamentalisms have arisen in nations beyond the scope of our inquiry, such as Egypt and Algeria, or many other places in the Muslim world. In the case of the United States, the tensions became unbearable in a number of Protestant denominations, when fearful but still aggressive leaders began to exploit the situation. The discontented group that became fundamentalists first began to make radical appeals to imagined pasts or pasts that they considered the majority could not or would not wish to retrieve. Leaders emerged who gave voice to the discontent and to organize the dissenters. In the case of Baptists and Presby-terians in America, these first called themselves "fundamentalists." They had two especially distinguishing features. First, they believed that they must, as one of them put it, "do battle for the Lord." Second, the arms they would use to fight off the moderates were appeals to doctrines that they regarded as fundamental.

Not always was doctrine the central theme. In Islamic cultures such as during the formation of the Muslim Brotherhood in Egypt in the same period, the issue came to be the application of the most strict laws drawn not so much from the Qur'an as from shari'ah, a body of laws which Muslims regard as rooted in the Qur'an and the Hadith of the prophet Mohammed. Decades later, when the mod-ern nation of Israel was forming, small Jewish fundamentalist move-ments like Gush Emunim broke with ultra-orthodoxy and found their fundamentals in the story, or to be precise, in ancient scriptural stories, which, they claimed, found the Lord deeding the land of Israel eternally to Jews. It is easy to point to similar developments, particularly in India, on Hindu and Buddhist soil, also in the same period.

While other religious fundamentalisms make less of story than do Jews, in some ways each company of strangers is a product and producer of stories. This is their strength and their bane for synthesizers and harmonizers. Jeffrey Stout has spoken clearly to this:

> People make their own history, though not under circumstances of their own choosing. The characters in our historical narratives are not concepts, like *scientia* and *opinio*, or domains of culture, like morality and religion, or historical forces, like differentiation and secularization. They are people, situated in circumstances that have conceptual as well as other dimensions, struggling to respond to these circumstances with the means at their disposal.[21]

The fundamentalisms were essentially movements of reaction against the conservatives and moderates, which means against those who they thought were compromising to the point of becoming corrupt. So they had to mobilize. At first, many did this by withdrawing from the public scene, since the creation of boundaries was important to them. Their withdrawal was not of old-fashioned conservative sorts, as typified earlier in the Western world by sects such as the Old Order Mennonites, the Amish, and the like. Old-fashioned conservatives basically wanted to be left alone. They wanted the world to pass them by and leave them free to follow their disciplines and practices.

The majorities and ruling powers in churches and in some nations recognized that fundamentalists in their reaction were potential or actual aggressors. That is, their retreat was strategic. They might want to be left alone for a period, but their larger design was to retake the polity in church or state, which they felt had belonged to them. They were found to be strangers, but they made claims that they were properly the belongers, as they followed the Bible and stood on the bedrock of early American founders. The established church members, now the belongers, saw the fundamentalists as strangers, intruders.

Decades later, when some of these fundamentalists outside the United States turned militant and engaged in warfare and terrorism, departments of state and mass communicators found themselves asking what was behind the fundamentalist aggressions. No single plot line covers them all, but there were often common features.

When two Muslims, one fundamentalist and the other not, or two Baptists, one fundamentalist and the other not, encounter each other intellectually and give expression to their disparate worldviews, they are manifestly both strangers to the other. One party will claim the rights of belonging because of its priority or size or religious correctness. In any case, the two factions quickly grow distant. Lonnie Kliever described these "two different worlds" and located them inside pluralism:

> Pluralism is the existence of multiple frames of reference, each with its own scheme of understanding and rationality. Pluralism is the coexistence of comparable and competing positions which are not to be reconciled. Pluralism is the recognition that different persons and different groups quite literally indwell irreducibly different worlds.[22]

Ambiguities of Adaptation: Muslim and Jewish

Adapting to the pluralist situation can be difficult among groups that have not long had the experience of a democratic polity or do not live in a liberal, open society. Non-Muslims in Western Europe, the British Isles, and North America have paid close attention, for example, to the way Muslims in their midst have struggled to find a place in the settings that are new for them. A case study will provide a window on such a struggle over the concept of fostering openness.

60

The Place of Tolerance in Islam is an important book occasioned as a defense by some Muslims against charges that intolerance is integral to Islam.[23] Abou El Fadl, who teaches law at UCLA, had been caught in a squeeze between critics of Islam who charge it can never be tolerant and critics in Islam who charge Abou El Fadl with compromising its essence. They insist that it *must* be intolerant. He summarizes the militant enclave view of "Muslim puritans" of today. "They display an intolerant exclusiveness and a belligerent supremacy vis-à-vis the other." For them, "Islam is the only way of life, and must be pursued regardless of its impact on the rights and well-being of others." He mentions their referring to strangers as *kuffar*, *munafiqun*, and *fasiqun*, which means infidels, hypocrites, and iniquitous. While relative tolerance and absolute intolerance have appeared at various times and places in Islamic history, Islam is now going through a major and novel shift. Its civilization has crumbled, and major traditional institutions that were agents of orthodoxy have been marginalized and often dismantled. Part of the problem came from the takeover of religious endowments (*awqaf*) in most Muslim countries, where the clergy have been co-opted. Spiritual anarchy resulted, and Wahhabi and Salafi creeds came to be used in attempts to fill vacuums in spirituality.

Abou El Fadl details the interpretation of intolerance, showing how radicals back their approach with selective quotes from the Qur'an, such as "O you who believe, do not take the Jews and Christians as allies. They are allies of each other, and he amongst you who becomes their ally is one of them. Verily, God does not guide the unjust" (Qur'an 5:51). They follow this with another verse that impels them to fight the unbeliever "until there is no more tumult or oppression, and until faith and all judgment belongs to God" (Qur'an 8:39). The extremists also cite: "Fight those among the People of the Book [Jews and Christians] who do not believe in God or the Hereafter, who do not forbid what God and His Prophets have forbidden, and who do not acknowledge the religion of truth – fight them until they pay the poll tax [*Jizyah*] with willing submission and feel themselves subdued" (Qur'an 9:29). That is all the charter they feel they need, says Abou El Fadl.

Over against such advocacies, Abou El Fadl provides contexts for those harsh texts and then supplies counter-texts also from within the Qur'an. Some of these merely praise diversity as a product of divine creation: "O humankind, God has created you from male and female and made you into diverse nations and tribes so that you may come to know each other. Verily, the most honored of you in the sight of God is he who is most righteous" (Qur'an 49:13). Similarly, "If thy Lord had willed, He would have made humankind into a single nation, but they will not cease to be diverse" (Qur'an 11:118–19.) More remarkably, some passages imply that there can be more than one path to God:

> To each of you God has prescribed a Law and a Way. If God would have willed, He would have made you a single people. But God's purpose is to test you in what he has given each of you, so strive in the pursuit of virtue, and know that you will all return to God [in the Hereafter], and He will resolve all the matters in which you disagree. (Qur'an 5:49)

Even more remarkably:

> Those who believe, those who follow Jewish scriptures, the Christians, the Sabians, and any who believe in God and the Final Day, and do good, all shall have their reward with their Lord and they will not come to fear or grief. (Qur'an 5:69; 18:29)

Over against these, the most frequently quoted passages legitimating aggression against unbelievers have to do with one dimension of jihad. Abou El Fadl recognizes that reformist Islam has to reckon with such texts. The Qur'an is emphatic: "There is no compulsion in matter of faith" (see Qur'an 2:256; 10:99; 18:29.) Abou El Fadl insists that Islam has no tradition of holy war. Jihad means no more than to strive and struggle for a just cause. Holy war (*al-harb al-muqaddasah*) is not in the Qur'an or classic Islamic interpretation; war is never holy; it is justified or not, no more. The Qur'an can even picture the Muslim combatant being on the unjust side!

Some of his critics, for example Milton Viorst, admit that Abou El Fadl has done well with the problem of Wahhabi extremism, but does not do justice to the way Islam as a whole has not let the texts that allow for openness to penetrate and shape their societies. Sohail H. Hashmi agrees with Viorst, that exclusivity and tolerance are virtually the norm in Islamic societies and traces the ways in which throughout history some mainstream Muslim commentators have "problematized" the very open texts Abou El Fadl cites. From the left, Tariq Ali faults Abou El Fadl for rendering the issue too theological, and insists that we must look at the lived life of the three monotheisms to see the source of the contemporary problem. "Priests and mullahs are no different. Nor are their followers. The fanatical Jewish settlers in Palestinian lands and the followers of al-Qaeda have much in common." For him, religion is epiphenomenal, an add-on to political and economic issues from and after Cold War days; the "international community" must address their anxieties and problems, and they will find interpretations of religion useless.

A Pakistani strategist, Abid Ullah Jan, shows how hard it will be for the Abou El Fadl's to make their way. His essay on "The Limits of Tolerance" makes that clear. He faults entirely not Wahhabi extremism but the Western quest for dominance, as in Algeria, Kashmir, Chechnya, in the United Nations, and by imposing sanctions on Iraq, Iran, Libya, Sudan, Pakistan, and Afghanistan. In an *ad hominem* attack he accuses "revisionist interpreters of Islam like Abou El Fadl" of trying to fill a vacuum of religious authority and faults him for rejecting Muslims who come to "highly exclusionary conclusions." Abou El Fadl should not mourn for a lost "pluralistic and unusually tolerant" Islam of the past, because Islam of the present is uncommonly tolerant of other peoples and religions. Predictably, he then attacks Israel and what it does to Palestinians. Ullah Jan utterly rejects Abou El Fadl's hint that there may be many paths to salvation (Qur'an 5:48 and 5:69), and counter-quotes these passages within the boundaries that the Qur'an draws in reference to *deen*, the overall belief system; *shari'a*, the law or way; and *minhaj*, approach.

At this point the debate parallels in logic and fervency that between pluralistic-minded Christians and exclusivists. Qur'an 3:85: "And whoever seeks a religion other than Islam, it will never be accepted of him, and in the Hereafter he will be one of the losers." Ullah Jan all but blames the current troubles on tolerance-minded Muslims, who overlook the injustices done to Muslims and thus implicitly justify what the West in its quest for dominance has done.

Stanley Kurtz enters the fray by scoring Abou El Fadl for trying to do justice to social historical settings instead of the text itself. In doing so, he stoops low as "a secular social scientist" who stands outside of tradition or even lower, in Kurtz's snide phrase, to the "sort of approach [that] may be popular at liberal divinity schools and departments of religion at American universities," but it is useless, he contends, because what he presents would have no appeal for Middle Eastern Muslims. Fundamental social change in uprooted and overpopulated poor Muslim areas must come, not "innovative textual interpretation."

Finally, for our purposes, R. Scott Appleby says that Abou El Fadl's text on tolerance in Islam is "who he is, and what he has been willing to stand for in the court of public opinion (at no small threat to his own well-being." The vital question is not "who ought to lead" but "how can qualified jurists, religious scholars, and leading intellectuals like Abou El Fadl regain a place of authority of the masses within the house of Islam?" Abou El Fadl did suffer a great deal; there were threats on his life, and he needed special protection. His case, which I have dealt with at some length, shows how difficult it is to move from the belonger/stranger dialectic even in a congenial pluralist climate like that of the United States.

Some Jewish scholars are wary about tolerance. They see it as a virtue too weak to be of help in improving relations among faith communities or to help their group retain boundaries and loyalty. The American Jewish community is divided over the subject, having been a beneficiary of tolerance, about which it remains ambiguous.

Tolerance has lost its vigorous connotations and now is seen by many as weak and wishy-washy. It is the faith of those who believe little and lightly, and ask you to do the same, so you can meet with each other at low risk, say the critics.

An alert against trying to make modern heroes out of ancient figures by uprooting them from their communal context inspires concern among some Jewish articulators. Letting one speak for many, I will turn to Jacob Neusner's essay on the subject, where he criticizes the disembodied notion of tolerance:

Tolerance does not suffice. A theory of the other that concedes the outsider is right for the other but not for me invokes a meretricious relativism that religious believers cannot really mean. Religions will have to learn to think about each other not merely to tolerate the other as an unavoidable inconvenience or an evil that cannot be eliminated . . . They face the task of thinking, within their own theological framework and religious system, about the place within the structure of the other outside of it. And that is something no religion has ever accomplished up to this time.[24]

For the Christian case, Stephen R. Barton, who cites Neusner, argues "we do not do the cause of a proper tolerance and a proper intolerance any favors if we harness Jesus or Paul or early Christianity to the bandwagon of post-Enlightenment secular individualism and pluralism." Such harnessing cuts off moderns from the roots – spiritual, interpretive, and ecclesial – that feed the Christian ethic of neighborly love. As this book contends, it also cuts off the truth claims of a world religion which, by its very distinctiveness and particularity, has made a significant contribution to a right understanding of tolerance and to the possibility and practice of different peoples living together in harmony, a harmony based upon faith in and faithfulness to the one true God.[25]

Jews by and large combine a great concern for the particularity of their view with a somewhat more generous approach to non-Jews whom they do not try to convert. Sometimes Jews put it this way when asked whether Jews believe non-Jews will be saved. They answer to the effect that Jews did not believe the world would be saved if everyone were converted to Judaism. But they did believe that it would *not* be saved if Jews were not faithful to the covenant.

Something deeper, richer, and more reliable than mere tolerance must come into play when dealing with the menace of the stranger. Introducing transcendent or religious questions into the civil scene or recognizing that they are there, troubling though they be, advances the discussion of dealing with diversity. Thus, Protestant theologian Reinhold Niebuhr wrote of a religious approach to the issue:

> This solution makes religious and cultural diversity possible within the presuppositions of a free society, without destroying the religious depth of culture. The solution requires a very high form of religious commitment. It demands that each religion, or each version of a single faith, seeks to proclaim its highest insights, while yet preserving an humble and contrite recognition of the fact that all actual expressions of religious faith are subject to historical contingency and relativity. Such a recognition creates a spirit of tolerance, and makes any religious or cultural movement hesitant to claim official validity for its form of religion, or to demand an official monopoly for its cult. Religious humility is in perfect accord with the presuppositions of a free society.[26]

In the course of ensuing chapters we shall move toward advocacy of hospitality, not tolerance, as an instrument or means of dealing more justly and with more potential of satisfying the interests of the faiths in collision and those who surround them and are affected by their interactions. For all such dealings, a pluralist polity has to be developed and ensured, as we shall soon see.

4

The Pluralist Polity

The presence of religious individuals or communities who are strangers under roof, next door, down the block, within the nation, and across the globe necessarily evokes a vast range of responses. The setting for these responses in our time almost universally comes with the label "pluralism." Definitions of the term vary widely, and one can often deduce the ideology of the definers by examining the descriptions of it that they offer. A late arrival in the vocabulary stock of the public – it has been in use in its present sense only a half-century – the concept stands in need of defense both against its enemies and its friends.

For and Against Pluralism

Its enemies dismiss it for contradictory reasons. To them, devotion to it is a fad that soon will pass or it is an idea whose time has gone. However much many would like to dismiss talk of it, it remains urgent. Issues having to do with religious integrity, neighborliness and civility, higher quality argument, the search for justice, and the avoidance of war are among those that relate to the ways people deal with pluralism. How people make decisions in its context is fateful in a world where people of various faiths are poised to jostle each other. It also demands examination because of the ways many use it to trivialize questions of commitment in matters of faith.

For many, any recognition of pluralism beyond noticing the fact of diversity will contribute to relativizing religion, morality, and government. Robert Kane speaks for those who see both secularization and the plurality of religions as "challenges to the spiritual center" of life in a society. He has presented the problem of a pluralism that veers into relativism with an example from popular culture:

> In a world of conflicting religious voices and texts, each claiming to speak from the divine point of view, [the path to finding an absolute point of view] is clouded; and it is further clouded by the secularization of modern life which leads to suspicion of sacred books, prophets, and churches of all kinds . . . When Archie Bunker [lead character in the television series *All in the Family*] was asked how he knew a certain message he had received had really come from God, he replied, "because God has one of those voices you never forget." The laughter of the audience made it unnecessary to express the response of a secular culture: "How did you know it was God the first time around?"[1]

Not assuming that my mere statement of what some of these features of pluralism are can itself be uncontroversial, I shall set forth those that are basic to this manifesto, and will elaborate upon them in subsequent pages.

Diversity or Pluralism?

From the first it is important to emphasize that pluralism, including religious pluralism, is not the same thing as diversity. Having diverse voices often in contention is a condition that calls for a polity, a network of policies and practices that has come most often to be described as pluralist. By a polity I mean simply any form of political organization, particularly in this case, one set forth constitutionally or that takes the form of a republic or a democracy. Mere diversity is not a synonym for pluralism, since it simply results from an obvious observation: "There are a lot of different things – races, ethnic groups, classes, peoples, interests, and religious communities hereabouts."

The people who make up these interests make news in the twenty-first century because of contentions among religious groups. In that picture all may be seen as being in conflict with each other, Hobbesian style. They live out their nasty, brutish, and short lives in ways that best help people pursue the interests of their group and try to gain advantage over others. On the other hand or in another vision, they may be largely at peace with each other, perhaps living in what is sometimes called pluralistic ignorance. They may have a dim awareness of the presence of others who believe and practice differently than they. But they live their own lives on a course that allows them to remain ignorant or indifferent.

Such belongers may live in a kind of psychic cocoon, choosing there to remain sheltered from others. They live in the midst of diversity, but we would not call their fabric of relations pluralism. However, when they do become aware and find the presence of others as having import, they cannot pretend their way back into such ignorance. So when persons or groups come to an awareness that the presence of others who are strangers will endure and that they will have some impact on each other, it is important to contemplate and fabricate some means for their relating.

Before passing over completely from the subject of mere diversity to pluralism as a polity and a framework for action, I want to pay attention to a very credible presentation of the case for choosing to focus on diversity. While moved by many of the critiques and proposals in the work, I see no need for the terminological shift proposed, and picture confusion should one elect to follow it. The book is James B. Wiggins' *In Praise of Religious Diversity*.[2] His comprehensive understanding that religious pluralism always calls for an explicit interpretive method and demands a practical commitment relates to a theological pluralism that is not our main topic. In the present volume, pluralism does incorporate an awareness of the diversity Wiggins celebrates, but then the discussion moves on to reflection on pluralist polity. Such pluralism remains a way of organizing life and encouraging an ethos to develop concurrently. What one might conceive or effect in the face of pluralism will await discussion in the last chapter.

A Modest Description of Pluralism

The various pluralist proposals and practices on display today manifest what people opt to *do* with the fact of diversity. What follows is a modest description, if not a formal definition, of pluralism.

Having devoted much of my vocation and many professional energies to the study of "public religion," with a specialty in researching and writing about pluralism, I have had to find condensed (call them "nutshell") ways to conceive of it and to speak about it in various publics. American religious historians are called to examine how in one polity, that of the United States, people have transacted with each other and dealt with issues amid diversity, as they fumbled their way into recognized and realized pluralism. Most of us then go on to ask what this recognition and realization mean for the interpretation of any particular faith among the many faiths. Sometimes I have been given the opportunity to tell stories of all this at book length, always along the way finding it necessary to define what I mean by pluralism.

The religiously informed civic pluralism that is my subject differs from either theological pluralism or turning pluralism itself into a theological theme. I have located pluralism in the sphere of politics, not metaphysics, though admitting that politics, like everything else that is serious, has a metaphysical grounding. The civic pluralism that concerns me relates more to practical adjustments in ways of life and then in theology. By locating it in politics I have to say of it what Bernard Crick said of politics itself, that it "does not claim to settle every problem or to make every sad heart glad." Further, it is "not religion, ethics, law, science, history, or economics; it neither solves everything, nor is it present everywhere . . . Politics is politics."[3] Pluralism is pluralism.

Arguments over pluralism often tempt all sides to hyperbole. Joel Belz, in a conservative evangelical magazine, *World*, called pluralism a "false deity" on the American scene. But if he overheated the rhetoric, so did his critic James Taranto of the *Wall Street Journal's* OpinionJournal.com, who wrote: "To the ranks of anti-American Christians we can add Joel Belz of *World* magazine, an evangelical weekly":

> Our real beef, though, is with Belz's apparent opposition to pluralism. If there is a quintessential principle that sums up the meaning of America, pluralism is it – and religious pluralism in particular. It is pluralism that allows everyone from evangelical Protestants to Catholics to atheists, from Mormons to Muslims to Jews, to live in the same cities and towns, free of the religious wars that divide such places as the Middle East. To be against pluralism, it seems to us, is to be against America itself.

When Belz took his turn he defined theological pluralism, not civil pluralism:

> The pluralism which I call a false god is pluralism which suggests that all religions are equally true or valid. When pluralism moves beyond everybody's right both to believe and even to propagate that belief peacefully, and then also argues that none of those beliefs is more true than any other of those beliefs – then something that started off as very good has become a false god.[4]

While we will discuss later some ways in which committed believers may reckon with the consequences of the pluralist reality and particularly its polity, there is no effort at this point to develop "a theology of religions" or "a theology of pluralism."

Any expert at employing a hermeneutics of suspicion, it is true, can unearth buried philosophies under even the most modest assumption that pluralism should be discussed at all. Discussing it positively brings with it the presupposition that a republic is not necessarily designed to thwart the will of God or compromise the teachings of

Jesus or Mohammed. At this point, to start the discussion of how we deal with the manifest variety of strangers' religions, we have to be practical and venture forth with some not very weighty sounding commonsense definitions.

What is pluralism, as in religious pluralism? Minimally, it is helpful to begin with "structural pluralism," wherein "society is understood to be made up of competing or perhaps complementary spheres," including religion, ethnicity, and government.[5] It is hard to become more modest and parsimonious about defining pluralism than that.

In varieties of audiences and readerships, seminars and forums, I have found most effective the use of a metaphoric approach drawn from the always readily accessible world of sports. I apologize for the un-philosophical and weightless sound of it, but it can bear philosophical weight and prompt satisfying historical inquiry. Here are the four main elements in pluralism:

Conditions
"Any number can play"
A considerable number does play
There are at least minimal "rules of the game"
The game develops an observable ethos

To elaborate. First: "Any number can play." At this point it is not necessary or possible to determine who authorizes or allows for the playing. We need only recognize here that permission may come from many sources and will develop on diverse grounds. Whatever these may be, they include the right or encouragement to recognize these diverse elements. In the circumstances of religious pluralism these begin as strangers to each other, but they share a playing field, a space, which somehow becomes a host place.

Second: "A considerable number does play." If circumstances prevail where only one individual is being religiously active, we would not speak of pluralism but of solitaire. And where only one group is on the scene there is again obviously no reason to speak of pluralism. If someone has a formal and legal monopoly, no matter how vigorously the dissenters may protest and act against it, as they might in the case of authoritarian regimes that exploit one religion, they are not helping constitute a pluralist situation. The fact that exceptional persons and groups have to be called dissenters means that someone in that polity enjoys a legitimated monopoly, however gained and held.

Double that one: a political entity which includes only two sets of strangers cannot be described as pluralist. While two is both "plural" and is part of the "any number" who can play, a situation in which only two are present and in conflict means potential warfare, not a civil working out of ways for citizens of a nation to live with difference. Perhaps we should say "any number more than two can play." All this recalls Voltaire's aphorism which James Madison liked to quote: "If one religion only were allowed in England, the Government would possibly become arbitrary; if there were two, they would be at each other's throats; but as there are such a multitude, they all live happy and in peace."[6] Any size of "multitude" larger than two will do.

A colonial empire in which one religion was established and favored by law did not concern itself with recognizing pluralism so long as two equal powers or only one dissenting force challenged it. When the number of groups grew, the time came for people of foresight to do something about the presence of the many, and their means of coexistence. Medieval Catholic leaders were aware that, hidden in the mountains, an occasional small protest group like the Waldensians might exist. The authorities would make every effort to deal with the strangers in their place, but they would never recognize that they had any other assignment than to try to silence, disperse, or extirpate them. There can be legal privileging of a faith community, such as Anglicanism in Britain, but there cannot be effective monopoly as a context for pluralist expression.

Third: "There are at least minimal 'rules of the game.' " These differ from nation to nation. In the United States the basic rules were confined to twenty words in Article VI of the Constitution and the sixteen words in the First Amendment. First, the Article reads: " No

73

religious Test shall ever be required as a Qualification to any Office or public Trust under the United States" and then, in the First Amendment, "Congress shall make no law respecting an establishment of religion or prohibiting the free exercise thereof."

Of course, these assurances of rights that make room for developing pluralism had to be worked out in constitutions of the several states for fifty years after Independence, down to 1833, when Massachusetts voted out the last colonial establishment. Even more emphatically, the United States Supreme Court interpreted and applied these thirty-six words of the Constitution and the Amendment in ways that unleashed the force of law, however they interpreted it. European nations that once employed law in attempts to expunge forces that made for pluralism now have moved toward disestablishing, at best privileging, or ignoring the voices and power of religious groups. Similar processes have developed also in many Asian nations, as well as in Africa and Latin America.

Many shadings color the experience of pluralism in diverse nations. Thus citizens of Israel are beneficiaries of freedom of choice in many respects. However, the legal favor given the Orthodox rabbinate has led to some restrictions. Thus the Church of Jesus Christ of Latter-day Saints had to agree not to proselytize if it wanted a place there. Israeli Jews can belong to any number of Jewish groups – movements which often contradict each other. Residents there may turn out to be, more rarely, Muslim or Druse or Christian. So diversity exists, but not in a fully defined civil pluralist polity. Only children born of Jewish mothers or only those Jews that were converted by Orthodox rabbis have full privileges. They are the belongers. Thus marriage and divorce laws favor one kind of established Judaism. Still, most observers would think that the protection of enough "rules of the game" does exist to legitimate the describing of Israel as pluralist.

The United Nations Declaration of Human Rights was a charter for freedom of religion and a legitimating of pluralism. Most nations claim to ensure religious freedom, but many do not do so in practice. When it comes to enforcing laws guaranteeing religious freedom,

74

UN powers are limited. So, for the present, the nation-state is the largest and most efficient agent for developing and enforcing such rules of the game.

On such terms and within a nation or state, strangers to a society of more or less homogeneous belongers are artists at learning what are the boundaries of expression. They need to learn who make up the various religious groups and to assess what kind of powers to command authority and compliance they possess. Also, to recognize rules of the game does not mean that all of them will always be fairly enforced, or that struggles to realize pluralism will ever be resolved to the satisfaction of all.

Fourth: "The game develops an observable ethos." José Ortega y Gasset has noted that cultures develop *vigencias*. These are binding customs based on no written or at best on highly diffuse written sources. The translator of a book by a scholar in Ortega's lineage, Julián Marías, defines this:

> *Vigencia* was originally a legal term and referred principally to laws and practices current and in force. Ortega and Marías use the term to describe laws, customs, usages, traditions, and beliefs that currently prevail in a given society or collectivity. *Vigencia* is related to that which has life (*quod viget*). There are social forces arising from many sectors of life and imposed on us without the intervention of our will. They are binding, impersonal forces that form the very fabric of the collectivity.[7]

In religion as in other realms, residents say that certain things are "done" or "not done" around here. Such customs become part of the ethos of dynamic and ever-changing societies. To get back to the sports metaphor that colors our description of pluralism: one doesn't "do" certain things about which the rule book of a game has nothing to say. You do not "do" them, that is, if you have a civil regard for competitors and audiences and if you want to encourage an opponent to play with you again. Thus in tennis, courtesy demands that a server not fire a second ball a split second after the first fails to go over the net. She is expected to allow a moment for the receiver to become poised and ready again. The rule book does not stipulate that one is to be legally penalized for such a discourtesy and uncivil action. A player instead becomes aware of the inconvenience, stigma, and threat to both civility and the quality of the game that go with such violations. Needless to say, not all "players" in the religion game will be concerned with "binding customs" and may in conscience even flaunt formal laws.

To take a controversial example of how people live with the ethos of pluralism in one particular setting and tradition: the rules of the game in a particular place may help ensure that anyone can try to convert anyone else. This is what freedom of religion means, as it allows citizens to make attempts to get others to change their religious commitment and community. The religiously uncommitted tend to be regarded as fair game for recruiters and proselytizers, though in their turn they may not welcome intrusions on their privacy. In the United States the Jehovah's Witnesses in 1940 won a case before the United States Supreme Court (*Cantwell vs. Connecticut* 310 US 696 (1940)) that ensured their freedom to play recordings of their messages in public settings. This was part of their efforts to get Christians and Jews and secular people to convert. Yet while most members of the less aggressive religious groups may chafe or be resistant to the insistent sound of the Witnesses' recorded message, nor welcome their persistent ringing of doorbells when canvassing to witness, they simply regard such Witnesses as nuisances who give religion a bad name, as violators of the ethos, not the law. They hope that one group's violation of the ethos of pluralism will not lead to a backlash by disaffected publics against all other religious endeavors.

The Muslim Circumstance

In many nations where the Muslim diaspora is relatively small, as in Western Europe and North America, some citizens in the non–Muslim majorities may speak uncivilly about the Islamic stranger next door or across the nation. They might allege, as some conservative evangelicals have done, not only that Islamic faith is wrong (or "evil") but also that Muslims owe fealty to a system that issues in terrorism around the globe. In the eyes of some, religious pluralism offers too much license to groups such as the Muslims, whom they abhor. But only if their abhorrence leads to illegal action, such as vandalism, will there be enforcement of "rules of the game."

Anti-Muslim zealots, however, may experience a backlash even from members of their own religious groups if they are too vocal and too extreme. They may consequently find it judicious and advantageous to mute their rhetoric. They would learn to do so in the interest of retaining some sort of civil society and, strategically, so as not to quicken reactions around the world that may harm their own larger mission in a global society. No civil authority or officer to police any violations of the ethos ordinarily does any guarding. Public opinion and the conscience of the individual and the group have to do the monitoring.

In those two paragraphs I have described two opposed approaches to Islam, which is on the most preoccupying scene of controversy. Non-Muslim people in the West are becoming increasingly familiar with the challenges of some Islamic critiques of and assaults on republics, pluralism, and discussion. An urgent question has arisen: *can* Islam contribute to and live with such a complex? Abdulaziz Sachedina claims it can, and at book length discusses Islamic roots of democratic pluralism. He knows that he is arguing against the grain of Western intellectual appraisals and the testimony of Muslim fundamentalists that supporting such pluralism is against the will of Allah and cannot be tolerated in Islamdom.

To follow all of Sachedina's revisitations of Qur'anic and other Islamic texts is not possible here. He details methods that he uses and wants others to use to disinter texts that advocate positive relations between Islam and pluralist polities and practices, and proposes "an Islamic theology of religions for the twenty-first century." Early on he describes his proposal:

I must retrace my steps to a God-centered public order in order to decode the Islamic endorsement of a pluralistic human society. There is an optimistic assumption in the divisions of the world into the domains of faith and disbelief (*dār al-īmān* and *dār al-kufr*) in Islam. It is founded upon extraordinary faith in the perfectibility of human beings. The only prerequisite for attaining that perfection is to "strive" (*jihād*) to "submit" (*islām*) to the inner intimations – the *fiṭra* – of natural religion. By implanting in humanity a natural predisposition to acknowledge the lordship of the Creator, God has made humans capable of responding to their original state when they come into contact with revelatory guidance through the prophets. This is the primary language of the Koran through which God provides the essential divine–human and inter-human connection.[8]

Sachedina is very critical of Islamic jurists, scholars, and people who have adapted to and fostered monolithic and repressive cultures, and shows an awareness of the difficulty contemporary Muslims world-wide would have recovering the roots he describes. Yet he concludes: "Islam's overlapping social and religious ideals can inspire the creation of pluralistic, democratic institutions in a best Muslim global community of the twenty-first century."[9]

My purpose in bringing up a topic that merits (and which Sachedina has given) book-length examination is not to state that his whole case has been made, or that acting upon it will be easy. There are two purposes for referring to him and it. First, to illustrate one of our main themes: that dealing with the stranger demands reexploration of one's own roots. Second, to suggest to those in the West who argue that Islam is by nature incapable of ever participating in democratic pluralist life, that they would be better off dealing with the Sachedinas, in endeavors to bring out the best instead of only advertising the worst in Islam's traditions, action which is the perfect counterpart to what Muslims do when dealing with Christian texts, roots, and outcomes.

The opposite strategy is the theme of many Western denunciations of Islam, typified in Robert Spencer's *Islam Unveiled*. He reads the Qur'an and other Islamic texts the way Muslim militants read the

Hebrew scriptures, as in the books of Joshua and Judges, where there are stories in which Yahweh commands genocide and the people of Israel endeavor to follow those commands. Again, we cannot pause to detail Spencer's arguments. Instead, merely to quote the chapter titles, all in question form, will suggest the plot. Needless to say, the answer to all but the one on the Crusades, which does not admit of a "Yes" or "No" answer, is "No"!

Is Islam a Religion of Peace?
Does Islam Promote and Safeguard Sound Moral Values?
Does Islam Respect Human Rights?
Does Islam Respect Women?
Is Islam Compatible with Liberal Democracy?
Can Islam Be Secularized and Made Compatible with the Western Pluralistic Framework?
Can Science and Culture Flourish under Islam?
The Crusades: Christian and Muslim
Is Islam Tolerant of Non-Muslims?
Does the West Really Have Nothing to Fear from Islam?

Given the simplicity and unambiguity of his "no's," one is left wondering whether it would ever pay for the non-Muslim majority in the West and Muslims to engage each other in conversation, interactions, negotiation, or anything but mutually preemptive strikes of warfare. Spencer concludes: "the wars will not end . . . It will clash increasingly with the weary secular powers that it blames for all the ills of the *umma*," unless "there is some wondrous intervention from the Merciful One." And that is something that Spencer does not envision or permit to enter his plot, nor is it figured into statecraft. The fact that so many Spencers (and their analogues in militant Islam) are in positions of power suggests how difficult it will be for any measures short of warfare to be enacted.[10]

After reading a defense of Islamic potential for pluralism and an attack, root and branch, against the possibility of there being such a potential, we are left to ponder again the issue of conversion as a means of theoretically reducing two faith communities to one. As of now, efforts by either religion add to the collisions among faiths that do occur when a group, pushing the limits of "binding custom" in the interest of expressive faith, sets out deliberately to try to uproot believers from within communities other than their own.

When the subject comes up, some fear negative reaction or disruption of civil peace, as when a militant Christian evangelist holds rallies, makes pitches, and broadcasts appeals for everyone unsaved, now including the Jew, to be saved. Jews will react negatively in defense of their community against such subversion by strangers. Whenever the goal of an evangelizing endeavor explicitly includes the effort by almost any means to invade the life of another community and to draw recruits from it, the aggressive group is testing the limits of the ethos of pluralism, as it is free to do in liberal societies.

A case study: the best-known evangelist in the world for a half-century and more is Billy Graham. His gospel contends that salvation is realized and effected only through Jesus Christ, and the mandate given him is to try to evangelize and convert anyone in range. It is hard to picture any of the evangelists, including Graham, who would be made unhappy when a Muslim or a Jew converts to Christianity. But in his last evangelistic campaign in heavily Jewish New York, the senior Graham wrote the rabbis to the reassuring effect that he was not targeting Jews for conversion. More ready to violate the ethos are groups like the Messianic Jews or Jews for Jesus, who do such targeting, not in violation of the rules of the game but of the ethos.

William Franklin Graham, son of the evangelist and a Christian activist and philanthropist himself, has targeted Muslims by singling them out for top-to-bottom attack. His father had profound differences with Islam, just as all Muslims have differences with Christianity. But the son spoke in sweeping, inclusive, and foundational terms when he regarded Islam at its root and in its branches to be a wicked and evil religion. His rhetoric was topped by even more rhetorically devastating expressions on the part of still more aggressive evangelists. While no authority had the power to shut them up, it was from within the evangelical community that effective voices appeared urging restraint. Violation of the ethos was a high risk in a time when national unity and understanding among the faiths needed promoting.

So far I have tried to establish that mere diversity is not the same as structural pluralism. Mere Balkanization, which would mean the division of territories that are adjacent to each other but separate in their laws and enforcements, does not constitute a pluralist society. Certain conditions have to be met before one can credibly call something religiously pluralist without creating confusion.

Pluralism in a Hierarchy of Values

We have not yet here located pluralism within a hierarchy of values or observations about human behavior, as the aggressive evangelizers have done. They serve as reminders of something that many in any religious community or what observers of human behavior regularly note. That is: supporting religious pluralism is *not* for everyone the highest, deepest, and most expansive value in religion. In the words of Dietrich Bonhoeffer, it belongs to the "penultimate" matters of life, not the ultimate.

To those hostile to all religion or those indifferent to its local forms, it may well be that religious pluralism, related as it is to religious liberty and the freedom to be non-religious, *is* an ultimate. They ask, what deeper commitment can one make than to ensure freedom of and from religion? However, for the religious to turn pluralism into a religious ultimate would undercut what Paul Tillich famously called "ultimate concern." It would represent idolatry, the placing of too much faith in the proximate, in a manifestly human invention. Fearful as the denial of religious pluralism can be, much of the human race got along without enjoying polities supporting religious pluralism for 160,000 years. Even the Western world did not have room for such real pluralism until the eighteenth century. To overvalue the penultimate is to bring expectations it cannot fulfill and frustration when it does not meet them.

81

While devotion to religious pluralism is not the highest priority of most individuals and is only one element in ensuring vitality in a republic, it does deserve constant attention, argument, and care. Pluralist societies do operate with explicit and implicit covenants, mainly civil, though they may be subject to philosophical and religious interpretation.

The political order is by definition fraught with potential for conflict and subject to outbreaks of such conflict. These occur within the rules of the game of politics. That collisions of religious faiths and communities figure prominently in the United States, yet in most years there are few dead bodies as a result of conflict among the faiths, puzzles many others. Some European nations see themselves as only reminiscently, nominally, and vestigially religious. Christianity in its various forms, they acknowledge, did contribute to their national formation, but it is not a vital agent today for ensuring the religious freedom of others.

In the United States religion is often visible in political affairs, but its location there is complicated by the fact that such a rich diversity of religious groups and voices is present that pluralism enters into the self-awareness of the nation itself. So citizens informally find ways to dull its force by developing a common, often called "civil," religion. Perceptive social thinkers such as Jean-Jacques Rousseau and Emile Durkheim discovered civil religions in complex and diverse societies. These, Durkheim argued, generate quasi-religious "collective representations" which help belongers both ground and celebrate what they presume to have in common. And these common elements are often rooted in implicit but still profound metaphysical commitments.

As societies such as the American drift from their religious roots and as their memory of traditional and particular faith commitments fades or communities disperse, they still engender some common approaches, as evidenced in the singing of the highly unspecific and nationally inclusive "God Bless America" in mixed public gatherings. Such singing may be a way many citizens have of overcoming the rawness of religious pluralism, but it is not an expression of that pluralism itself.

When the members of a host society who celebrate civil religion confront intense religious strangers, these groups appear to be unsettling, unpatriotic. Thus when Muslims in numbers of Western European nations increasingly made visible their celebration of Islamic tenets and Muslim practices, as they bannered central Islamic tenets and observed Muslim ceremonies, these seemed strange and thus ominous and even potentially destructive.

Pluralists on the Defensive Over "Tolerance"

Many citizens of republics have been stunned to recognize that pluralism and religious freedom are on the defensive in many parts of the world. They are so, too, when they are challenged from within such republics, when collisions among faiths occur or when people weary because of the inefficiencies of producing a single national ideology in the presence of legitimated religious diversity. Today, nowhere around the globe do religious groups that promote tolerance or reconciliation outpace or out-attract those that erect barriers against others, and in which the belongers are hostile to religious strangers. Those who think of themselves as having the main rights to belong may claim these as a result of their custodianship of many historical memories, through brute political power, or by portraying the strangers in negative terms. By and large, they prosper. Awareness of this spiritual economy is an element in the surprising rise of modern religious fundamentalisms and other militancies.

This points to a paradox in the whole concept of tolerance. As John Horton has written: "It is widely agreed that the core of the concept of toleration is the refusal, where one has the power to do so, to prohibit or seriously interfere with conduct that one finds objectionable."[11] Such conduct would mean worshipping a God other than one's own, or being an agent of a religion that tempts one to interfere. In other words, only the powerful are in a position to be called to be generous. But in pluralism where stranger meets stranger, to be called to tolerate may occur where there is not much

83

power except destructive potency, and where acts of toleration will be suppressed by those who exert majority power, that of the belongers.

Awareness of the success by anti-pluralists in our time prompts some to reexplore the strengths and weaknesses of many religious groups that had been promoting positive relations among religions. They are asking themselves, or being asked: Are they too tender minded? Are they fatally weak, in danger of being dissolved or ground up between more assertive forces, sacred and secular? Evidently no one can prosper religiously by trading on the liberal *Zeitgeist*. Working for civil peace and for concord across the boundaries of the faiths is less marketable than are aggressive religions. Of course, some counter-signs and some successes are evident, but for now one must say that those who appreciate republics cannot take them for granted. Nor can they coast as they relish and would strengthen the framework of religious pluralism.

Counsel for taking the first step in understanding pluralism will sound passive and soft in the ears of the assertive religionists. Yet it is hard to avoid the observation that everything begins with religious groups listening, inquiring, becoming aware of limits, engaging in self-criticism. It further means affirming the values of dissent, for those who promote positive relations among religions will be scorned by the larger company of belongers. They see dissent as militating against the health of the belongers and the qualities they bring.

Why there has been a retreat from placing a premium on understanding and common action among groups is puzzling to many. What went wrong to deny the dreams of those who pictured and worked for a new millennium of positive interactions? Why do the hard-edged, hardlined religious groups prosper? Both humanists and people of religious faith who believed that, after the Enlightenment, reason and progress and science would dominate, are now bemused by the power of these counter-forces. There are reasons for them to begin to learn by being self-critical, something at which people of moderate or liberal impulse are derided for being good at.

84

Many features of their own movements have been contributors to their own problem. First, many of them put too much faith in bureaucratic rationality and paid too little attention to the demands of the heart. Thus they lost out to those who understood passions more than they did. In the twentieth century, the great Christian councils of churches within nations and globally are often rightfully perceived as guilty of being remote from constituents and self-preoccupied with their commissions, committees, and compacts.

Second, some of the weakness in such movements may have come from a failure of nerve among intellectuals, including political and religious leaders. They were not always ready to examine their own half-disclosed commitments – for example, to philosophies that promote tolerance – but took form in movements that themselves displayed too many evidences of intolerance. When we were studying fundamentalisms around the world, all of them typed as being "on the right," critics with some justification pointed us to fundamentalisms on the left, among the very people who in opposing standard-brand fundamentalism kept seeing themselves as advocates of tolerance, openness, and empathy.

Third, there is some justification in the charge that defenders of pluralism often were not content with minimal and straightforwardly practical approaches to the politics of pluralism. Some moved beyond this to smuggle in philosophies that themselves acquired a kind of religious cast. As the religiously intense defended the philosophical foundations of their outlooks, they were quick to attack philosophical foundations as cherished by advocates of pluralism.

Many advocates of tolerance had faith in the power of non-religion to provide all the foundation or network a society needed or that its members craved. Since intense religion contributed to estrangement and, in extreme situations, to warfare, they argued that the way to limit the damage was to turn consciously to non-religion for support or mediation. Eliminate religion, they said, and the danger to civil order will have been cut off root and branch. That counsel got little hearing. While one may recognize some neutralizing affects attributable to indifference and secularization in European nations, conscious efforts to extirpate religion have not been successful. They have generated only more discontented and militant tribes of hardliners.

Thus the Soviet-bloc nations after World War II adopted anti-religious policies instituted by the Leninist revolution in Russia in 1917. In the end, they only succeeded in having anti-religion acquire major characteristics of religion. Their institutions looked similar to those of repressive religions. When in 1989 the Iron Curtain was torn down, though the companies of religious believers had been forced into hiding or very quiet observance for seventy-two years, they all had endured and had seen the rise of new faiths as well. When anti-pluralism turned into anti-religion, vacuums and voids got created and state ideologies of a religious character filled them. When after 1989 the anti-religious Eastern bloc intellectuals saw their empire implode, they had to observe that it had been outlasted by Muslim nations in Central Asia and Jewish and Christian presences all over Russia and among its former satellites.

One brute fact with which the secularist has to reckon is that if one takes the whole globe into view, the notion of solving problems posed by religious pluralism by doing away with religion is fruitless. Religion around the world not only shows no signs of disappearing but instead is prospering, often in the most anti-pluralist forms. People in most societies show no sign of giving up their religious faiths. How they will channel their religious energies becomes the major issue. It is always harder to organize people around efforts to preserve and enlarge republican principles and associations than it is to form closed enclaves.

One may at the same time speak of the limits of secular forces and ideologies. But most of those who support religious pluralism are also quick to note that the secular envelopes of ideas surrounding our cultures, and the secular canopies of practices that enshroud them, will not go away. True, they may be altering their character in the face of challenges posed by militant religious groups. The publics on a global scale show less faith now than they did a half-century ago that humans are truly in control, veritably Promethean, and that they can rationalize their way through instruments of progress into some sort of religionless utopia.

What survives in liberal societies is a way of life often based on non-religious commitments. In a republic, for the majority, no other fabric than the one based on secular rationality serves to explain so many aspects of reality and make possible adjudication of controversies in medicine, law, and politics. But few sign on to formal humanist manifestos. Let the pluralist ways of life and justifications for them remain informal, and let them lack their own articulators and proselytizers. They are likely to endure. Pluralists as well as secularists are less successful than members of formally religious communities at rendering their commitments into formal creeds and covenants.

You would think that the negative case against religion-gone-bad would carry the day. We have already noted that in our decades more conflicts and even more wars and more killings go on over clashes among faiths than in battles over territory, for revenge, or in vainglory. Add to this the psychic damage among victims where religious pluralism is absent, where coercion of faiths and ideologies prevails, or where those in power are coercive and abusive in the name of God, and the balance of favor apparently tips even more against religion as a whole.

How Pluralism Develops in the United States

A close-up of the scene in the United States, where pluralism is so rich and religions have prospered, can illuminate a view of experiences elsewhere. One of the clearest assertions of awareness that the United States was and would become an ever more pluralist society and that it needed rules of the game to go with it came in 1779, when Thomas Jefferson began promoting religious freedom in the colony of Virginia, where the decisive battle and breakthrough occurred. From the backwoods of the colony came cautionary and denunciatory words. In the *Virginia Gazette* a writer acknowledged that "Jews, Mohamedans, Atheists, or Deists" did have to be recognized as citizens, but they should not hold office or be free to promote their "singular opinions." And an Amherst County petition furthered the talk full of suspicion of the stranger: no Catholic, "Jew, Turk, or Infidel" dared hold civil or military positions. Lesson one for advocates: compacts or constitutions which would provide for pluralist polities have to anticipate enlargements of the scope of inclusion: Jews, Turks, and Infidels were not yet very visible parts of the scene in Virginia in the 1770s.

Lesson two, illustrated from history: as far as possible, avoid privileging particular faiths. Jefferson took up the issue when drafting the Virginia Bill for Religious Freedom that was passed in 1786. James Madison, who was to be central in the drafting of the Constitution, had resisted a proposal by some legislators that would have ruled the stranger out. They would do so in the name of the religion of belongers. He successfully argued against inserting "the words 'Jesus Christ' after the words 'our Lord'" in the preamble, because that would have meant "a restriction of the liberty defined in the bill to those professing his religion only." When that amendment was defeated, Jefferson declared that the defeat of that proposal proved that the lawmakers "meant to comprehend, within the mantle of its protection, the Jew and Gentile, the Christian and Mahometan, the Hindoo, and infidel of every denomination."[12]

Lesson three: in free societies the battle for religious liberty and the shape of pluralist polity is never ended. Madison, Jefferson, and the majority in the Virginia legislature did not have the field to themselves, and could not ensure the future. Take the instance of the Jews, who often had to fight in courts through the twentieth century for assurance that the rules of the game did not discriminate against them. Along the way voices like that of the leading rabbi Isaac Leeser in 1857 sounded a typical plaint for the Jews: "If we make all the noise in the world, and brag aloud after our heart's content, *we are yet strangers* in stranger lands."[13] The application of the rules of the game was still uncertain.

For all the struggles over the game of pluralism, the word itself rarely showed up in the century and a half after the Constitutional rules of the game became law. In 1924 a Jewish thinker, Horace Kallen, coined the concept of "cultural pluralism," but there was little follow-up use of the term. Reference guides to American periodical literature through the first half of the twentieth century locate the word very rarely, and never in the sense that it has in discussions of pluralist polities.

The first modern usage of the term applied to religion is referenced in the *Reader's Guide to Periodical Literature, 1951–1953. Christian Century* is an ecumenical weekly whose editors then still regarded Catholics as strangers in America. These editors, criticizing efforts by the Catholic bishop of Buffalo to help fund parochial education, headlined their editorial "Pluralism – National Menace."[14] The article reflected the magazine's concept of how two contenders fought for a place in one nation, but in the years that followed the usage broadened and the word pluralism came quickly to be accepted by the general public.

Few books in this period did more to frame the emergent concept of realized pluralism than Jewish sociologist and religious thinker Will Herberg's *Protestant, Catholic, Jew* in 1955.[15] Herberg was trying to account for a putative revival of religion in the "Eisenhower Era," a stir named after a president who gave encouragement to it. What we have called "civil religion" or "public religion" under a "sacred canopy" Herberg called "a civic faith." He observed that citizens chose to support a generic and single American way of life with sanctions and ceremonies grounded in their own particular faith communities. He did a great deal of generalizing in order to snuggle these into three clusters, and had to overlook many expressions of diversity within a pluralist polity while doing so.

At the same time, and suggesting how Catholicism was suddenly seen to be emerging in the American community, many of whose leaders and publics had rejected it a decade earlier, an important work appeared in 1960 by Father John Courtney Murray, SJ: *We Hold These Truths: Catholic Reflections on the American Proposition.*[16]

89

The book's first chapter was called "The Civilization of a Pluralist Society." Murray, as a Catholic, took up the problem of being strangers in society by quoting the second-century *Letter to Diognetes:* "Every foreign land is a fatherland and every fatherland is a foreign land" for Christians. The priest was trying to show in what ways the pluralistic civilization that the United States was intended to be could be a fatherland. It could be a home place for the Catholics who on philosophical and historical grounds should never even have been thought of as strangers in the first place. Making a major contribution to American pluralist reflection along the way, Murray was a realist about the American situation. He pointed first to a philosophical problem: "We have no common universe of discourse."

> In particular, diverse mental equivalents attach to all the words in which the constitutional consensus must finally be discussed – truth, freedom, justice, prudence, order, law, authority, power, knowledge, certainty, unity, peace, virtue, morality, religion, God, and perhaps even man. Our intellectual experience is one of sheer confusion, in which soliloquy succeeds to argument.

Murray spoke of Catholics, Protestants, Jews, and secularists as constituting "conspiracies," which meant that they "breathed together." He might have added Mahometans, Hindoos, and Infidels. They lived off stories with meanings so incommensurable that citizens had difficulty having and interpreting communal experiences. The stories, he wrote, "are so divergent that they create not sympathies but alienations as between groups." Murray therefore combined a Catholic judgment with a pluralist-based description in a famous summary:

> Religious pluralism is against the will of God. But it is the human condition; it is written into the script of history. It will not somehow marvelously cease to trouble the City.
>
> Advisedly therefore one will cherish only modest expectations with regard to the solution of the problem of religious pluralism and civic unity . . . But we could at least do two things. We could limit

90

the warfare, and we could enlarge the dialogue. We could lay down our arms (at least the more barbarous kind of arms!) and we could take up argument.

Even to do this would not be easy . . .

All this might be possible. It certainly would be useful. I venture to say that today it is necessary . . . Perhaps the time has come when we should endeavor to dissolve the structure of war that underlies the pluralistic society, and erect the more civilized structure of dialogue. It would be no less sharply pluralistic, but rather more so, since the real pluralisms would be clarified out of their present confusion.

The engagement Murray advocated had been developing for some years. Religious groups that were in conversation had worked out groundrules to contribute to its success. The favored term for this at the time was dialogue. More recently the term and concept of conversation parallels or replaces dialogue, which assumes a somewhat more formal discourse.

In many renditions, argument, the polemical approach, is guided by the answer. One antagonist has the answer to what is troubling and at issue, and she must convert, convince, silence, or defeat the other. Argument has its place in legislatures, courts of law, and universities, but skilled debaters can drive away the intimidated who bring questions or have unresolved issues. Conversation, on the other hand, is moved by the questions, and takes on something of the character of an inconclusive game. One does not hear claims such as "I sure won *that* conversation!" And conversation is especially appealing because it invites in on equal terms host and guest, belonger and stranger, the committed and the less committed, the informed and the less informed. Across the boundaries of faiths they have no referee or determiner of a winner, since the faiths do not begin by accepting the texts and traditions of the other as finally determinative for them, or even as an acceptable authority in the first place.

Paul Mozjes, speaking of dialogue in ways that inform our parallel, conversation, defined it in ways that can help clarify our project:

Dialogue is a way by which persons or groups of different persuasions respectfully and responsibly relate to one another in order to bring about mutual enrichment without removing essential differences between them. Dialogue is both a verbal and an attitudinal mutual approach which includes listening, sharing ideas, and working together despite the continued existence of real differences and tensions. Dialogue is a conscious process in which partners seek to give and take without recourse to force and intimidation.[17]

Herberg's tri-faith and Murray's four-conspiracies visions appeared narrow thanks to an explosion of interest in identities among subgroups of Asian Americans, African Americans, Native Americans, Latin Americans, and others, which led the public to have to deal with an ever more rich and complex pluralist scene. Added to the voices now being heard were new voices of immigrants, who brought their religion with them, especially after the then little noticed change in immigration laws in 1965 The change affected the United States in many ways and as much as the concurrent Civil Rights breakthroughs and commitment of troops to war in Vietnam. It certainly was responsible for the biggest change in the make-up of the population after the immigration laws of 1924 had closed the door to most peoples regarded as strangers.

Some newcomers were refugees, victims, and exiles from Southeast Asia after the Vietnam War. Others came across the Rio Grande from Mexico or by boat or plane from Africa and all of Asia. While many African-American blacks began to identify themselves with the Nation of Islam and later with orthodox Islam, immigrants from Muslim nations greatly swelled the Islamic population, presence, and power. Native Americans, who belonged from prehistoric times but were estranged even in the post-Constitutional era, spoke up and forced redefinition of their status.

The presence of all these peoples necessitated a fresh look at the working out of pluralism. In the language of our metaphor about games, now a greater number than before could and did play. They forced some adjustment of some rules of the game, and participated in developing a new ethos. Midwestern cities and small towns, often with the nudge and support of their churches, welcomed thousands of the newcomers, most of whom did not share "Judeo-Christian" faiths. Fargo, North Dakota, Cedar Rapids and Postville, Iowa and Lincoln, Nebraska were among the sites where the new accommodations to the pluralist mix were dramatically worked out.

In the new century, almost daily, the press provides a close-up of interactions in some American city or other. One example, chosen almost arbitrarily, is Lewiston, Maine, as featured in the popular press. Reporter Charisse Jones visited the small city which is, or was, 96 percent Roman Catholic. By 2003, 1,100 Somalis who settled there experienced unrest. A few of these Africans were attacked and more of them shunned, but they endure. Phil Nadeau, assistant city administrator, diagnosed the situation in terms congenial to our "stranger" thesis:

> I think the reluctance [on the part of many to welcome the newcomers] is the fear of the unknown. Something as simple as "Gee, this individual is Muslim. I hear they pray five times a day. Does that mean he has to get away from the cash register and pray every hour and a half while he's on his shift?" Those kinds of things.[18]

"Those kinds of things" were becoming so visible and plaguing that Mayor Laurier Raymond made national news by writing an open letter to Somali residents, urging them to discourage relatives from coming. In a follow-up, a white supremacist group, the World Church of the Creator, arrived to rally and stir hatred. City Councilman Roger Philippon said of local citizens, "I think a lot of people felt that they were probably very open and tolerant and maybe now realize the maybe they aren't quite so." But Jones noted that the trend toward more diversity was inescapable. At Lewiston, Bethlehem, Pennsylvania, Lowell, Massachusetts and similar fearful cities, immigrants fortuitously helped revive stagnant and even dying places. As reported by Jones, mixing basic humaneness with good coaching and economic incentives, many long-term residents of Lewiston worked to effect change and welcome the stranger.

France and Its Secular Kin

Meanwhile, on the international scene, France received much attention and approached crisis, especially since its secular laws and secular intentions left citizens unprepared for a new challenge as Muslims there became more visible, more articulate, and more threatening. Tom Hundley, a *Chicago Tribune* correspondent, told of tensions in the city of Lille. After the expulsion in Creil of three Muslim girls who wore outlawed headscarves to school, the French left and right, religious and non-religious, engaged in intense controversy. Headlined stories of headscarf-wearing women medical students who would not treat male patients led to more conflict. A juror in a court near Paris was dismissed because she started wearing a headscarf after she had been elected to the jury. The government had to intervene by creating panels to study and arbitrate. Are scarves religious symbols or practices? Courts have to decide. When President Jacques Chirac, who had appointed a commission to appraise the situation, sought legislation against the wearing of the veil, his words and acts led to more polarization among citizens.

At stake is the French invention of *laicite*, which in the French Republic has meant stipulations by political forces to religious authorities: hands off and stay at a distance from civil life. Bruno Bourg-Broc, a member of a school panel, spoke up: "We risk replying to one form of extremism with another. For me, *laicite* is mutual respect and tolerance," but ruling out headscarves "would appear as a declaration of war on Islam."

France is the most tense scene of conflict over religion and secularity in Europe. Jacqueline Cost-Lescoux, a political scientist on Chirac's commission, claimed: "The majority of the 5 million Muslims in France want to integrate. They welcome the freedoms they find here. But then there are the militants. They have their own agenda, and they are using this issue to see how far they can go."[19]

These expressions demonstrate that France is a classic case where strangers disturb an old synthesis. A story in the *Economist* of Aubervilliers also dealt with the controversy over headscarved girl students. The magazine featured young Lila Lévy-Omari, who said: "France is hiding behind the principle of secularism because Islam is new, and frightening. I am French, I was born in France. But what are the criteria for being French? Catholicism? It's as if, as soon as we're Muslims, we can't belong here."[20]

The stranger is also perceived and feared as someone who changes the familiar landscape itself. Craig S. Smith, reporting from Cergy Le Haut, France, quoted Jean-Marie Chaussoniére, an attorney there: "A big mosque can change the silhouette of a neighborhood and the character of a town . . . I'm afraid it will only invite extremists." She added, Muslim custom "isn't our patrimony."

Such attitudes can lead to attempts at excluding the stranger. Smith reported that in Sartrouville critics attacked the "Islamization" of the town and forbade the building of a mosque. Muslims had to worship in a existing secular building. The town quickly shut it down for safety violations. "It remains closed today."[21]

By the autumn of 2003 news from France as it dealt with the Muslim stranger attracted the attention of major media worldwide. The *Chronicle of Higher Education* headlined "Muslims Worry French Universities." Reporter Burton Bollag told of disruptions by Muslim students who claimed that some teaching was "un-Islamic," and that there was a high "degree of anxiety in France over the issue of Islamic fundamentalism at the universities."[22]

Reporter Elaine Sciolino in December of 2003 reported on a chartered panel that submitted a formal report to President Jacques Chirac calling for a law to ban "conspicuous" religious symbolism and garb among students in French schools. She provided perspective, reminding readers that France has a long tradition of separating religion from public life and drawing a sharp line between secularism and religion in schools and elsewhere:

> In one century, because of immigration, French society has become diverse in terms of its spiritual and religious aspect. The challenge today is to give space to new religions while at the same time to succeed in integration and struggle against political–religious manipulation.[23]

Meanwhile, a letter from the Council of Christian Churches, which is made up of Orthodox Christians, Protestants, and Roman Catholics, warned that banning the Islamic headscarf and similar religious symbols "would be felt as discriminatory." The council was speaking up in fear lest such a ban on Islamic symbols would mean the removal of the Christian cross in public settings.

While the faiths colliding in France centered on Islam and a form of secularism which official France regards "religiously," one might say, there and in other mainly European nations citizens were faced with the task of accommodating strangers with their unfamiliar faiths, meanwhile adjusting their concepts and practices of pluralism. They had some options, and exercised them in ways that deserve exposition, and will shortly receive it.

It would be injudicious of me to leave this discourse about dialogue and conversation without recognizing and anticipating a taunting critique. It goes something like this. Strategies centering on dialogue, conversation, and risking hospitality are luxuries in the wimpy and namby-pamby worlds of liberals in liberal cultures. They work to some extent, at least until *really* tested in protected pluralist societies, polarized and intense though their partisans be. Putting those strategies to work may have moderating and ameliorating effects where the stakes are not so high or the weapons so pointed as they are where most faiths collide. What good are they at the wall separating Israelis from Arabs, and what do they have to say to terrorists in a world of suicide bombing, where Shi'ite and Sunni Muslims, Kurds, and "Coalition forces of the West" are killing each other? Answer: very little. They come too little and too late, though, after all the deaths, those who survive and try to rebuild may well learn from such disarming techniques and models.

The point is to address experiences of "belongers" versus "strangers," where faiths are at issue, whenever breakdown in civility threatens, and wherever interfaith discourse and common action are still possibilities. That represents enough places and situations around the globe to warrant investment.

5

Living with a Pluralist Polity

In the literature and in the record of pluralist polities, three options for public life predominate.

First is for citizens, believers and non-believers alike, to relax with what I call *mere* pluralism. They are stunned by the suddenness of population changes. The neighborhood and the nation are not as familiar as they once were. Lacking a handle on the new situation, they find it hard to comprehend all the changes and leave the task of welcoming them to others. Too many Burmese in Baptist Texas, too many Muslims in Lutheran and Catholic Minnesota, too many Lubavitscher Jews in Postville, Iowa make for a bewildering presence; too many Muslims in France or Indonesians in Britain can overwhelm those who were belongers in such places.

Close our eyes, the relatively passive may decide, and the different people may go away. Someone else, somewhere else, they think, should take up the task of providing the theory and practices through which they can face diversity. If affairs continue to go well in their own front yards, they think change will remain remote. Merely say NIMBY, "Not in my back yard," they think, and maybe nothing will happen in their back yard. Assume that things will work out all right in the end. Divert attention. There are so many other things to do: get lost in business or gardening, go deep into their own religion and never be concerned with what happens outside their own sanctuary. The citizen who is content with mere pluralism looks out the window at the wide variety of clusters and soon pulls down the blinds.

The other extreme is to face a second construct, which I call *utter pluralism*. Citizens who make diversity their main subject of observation and experience have several choices. Some will embrace it, but others will run from it. In utter pluralist concepts and contexts, citizens may use the presence of the many peoples they observe in order to praise diversity, to call for delight in variety and choice, to experience the stranger as neighbor – and the more strangers the better! Or they may try to stand equidistantly from all options, while celebrating their presence.

The negative version of this distancing calls for belongers to bemoan what others have done to the society to which they had belonged. Just as the one who settles for mere pluralism does not intervene, so some celebrators or deplorers of utter pluralism choose to stand aside. The citizen who celebrates utter pluralism looks out the window, takes in the panoply of strange groups, gasps in awe at the variety, and lets it go at that.

The positive appreciation of utter pluralism leads some to say of the options the varieties of religion presents, "the more, the better," and move from one to another of these varieties as advocates of free choice in faith.

Citizens committed to the adventures that go with the third option, the pursuit and enhancement of *civil pluralism*, undertake tasks of observing, understanding, and contributing to its development. No less aware than the others of the potential for disturbance and disruption that strangers might bring, these citizens become agents of change, not passive bystanders. To understand them one must assess the reasons why many resist strangers in their groups and communities.

The very notion of affirming or celebrating pluralism is appalling to many belongers. Many believers among them fear what the presence of others will do to their own community and commitment. Assessing what potential effects pluralism may have on the growth and health of their own religion and tribe is a difficult and chancy affair. One set of sociologists comes up with data showing that church membership has prospered where diversity increases. Then another set faults the data and conclusions drawn from it.

Mark Chaves and Philip S. Gorski entered the conflict between the two camps, first quoting two contrary opinions. On one side is Daniel Olson: "It appears that North Americans are religious in spite of, not because of, religious pluralism." On the other side, Roger Finke and Rodney Stark observe: "Religious practice is strongly and positively associated with pluralism."

In the former camp are those who believe that the bewildering variety of options leads the citizens who make a choice among them to take them less seriously than they should. In the latter are those who make their judgment using rational choice theory and concepts of supply-side economics. In such cases, those one might name entrepreneurs or marketers of religion tailor their product to enhance their appeal for new members and more participation by existing ones. With all those options available, only with ingenious inventions to attract more, it is argued, more citizens than before are more religious.

After Chaves and Gorski weighed the evidence they offered as their grand conclusion that it is inadvisable to make a kind of "law" in which pluralism would in principle and practice clearly lead either to the prosperity or the decline of religion. "The evidence clearly shows," they write, "that any such general law, to be accurate, would have to be formulated with so many exceptions and qualifications that its claim to generality or lawfulness would be empty."[1]

As the two camps fight to a draw or fail to come up with arguments convincing to all, the realist does not wait for the outcome. Pluralism and the presence of religious strangers get blamed by one camp for many of the things that they observe as having gone wrong in their society. A vivid example that demonstrates public uncertainty about how to promote homogeneousness and consensus comes from the United States after 1962. That year Supreme Court rulings outlawed organized prayer and devotional activities in public schools. In *Engel vs. Vitale* and the next year in *Abington School District vs. Schempp*, the Supreme Court ruled in favor of those whom the majority of citizens, according to the polls, regarded as strangers. Some Jews, secular humanists, liberal Christians, and Protestant sectarians protested that having prayers stipulated or arranged by public school

administrators, or even making formal provision for these, represented a sort of establishment or privileging of religion.

Some of the fury – and it *was* and *is* fury – has been directed at
the members of the Supreme Court and the presidents who appointed
them. But those who are somewhat more sympathetic to the court's
reasoning note the fact that the justices are aware that great numbers of groups do not share the broad outline of religious faith with
those who have populated a state for a long period. Were it not for
these irritating and agitating strangers, the homogenizers think, schools
could do what they had done before: observe the holidays and
ceremonies of the majority faith, which many call by a name invented
in the twentieth century: the Judeo-Christian tradition.

The school prayer decisions were often seen by critics as an effort
to prevent that tradition from having an established or privileged
position in public places. In the most widely publicized case, Roy
Moore, before he became Chief Justice of the Alabama Supreme
Court, posted his own handcrafted version of the Ten Commandments on the wall of his judicial chamber. In 2003, after he became
Chief Justice, Moore arranged for the placing of a granite rendition
of the Commandments in the vestibule of the Supreme Court in his
state. Critics pointed out to him that the Ten Commandments were
not generic moral laws but were instead held by believers to be
utterances of the only God, a jealous God. The idea of employing
school property, personnel, and time to favor this God over against
other religious approaches by citizens and taxpayers forced Moore
to defend himself. He welcomed the challenge. When asked whether
this practice was fair, he answered that Alabama was not part of a
Buddhist or Hindu nation. It is a Judeo-Christian one, which meant
that adherents, who constituted a clear majority, had a right to spell
out the terms for what adorned the space that belonged to the whole
public, including all its minorities. When the US Supreme Court in
2003 ruled against Moore, he and his followers protested against
the voices of non–representative minorities – in other words, again,
strangers. The belongers were belligerent, vowed to fight another
day, and in a changing climate may win the day.

The strangers may further look repellent because those who regard themselves as privileged in the host culture fear that the strangers may succeed in efforts to convert members of the older and more homogeneous community. When members of a family rooted in a mainstream tradition convert to the Latter-day Saints, Jehovah's Witnesses, the Unification Church, or Buddhism, those who remain in the tradition find confirmation that the foreign can be alluring and beguiling. They might convert more. When through and after marriage the daughter of a Christian turns Muslim and raises the children of that marriage in Islam, many in the family and the circle of friends may be similarly repulsed. They try to isolate, quarantine, or expel the stranger.

Families or citizenries who "lose" someone through conversion recognize what social thinkers have long held. The apostate or renegade, for social, psychological, and often theological reasons, finds it important to be almost fanatically loyal to the new group at the expense of any ties to the old community. Social hatred, writes Georg Simmel, our guide through the thickets of pluralism, then "is directed against a member of the group, not from personal motives, but because the member presents a danger to the preservation of the group." Further, "the recall of earlier agreement" among those who had once belonged to each other, "has such a strong effect that the new contrast is infinitely sharper and bitterer than if no relation at all had existed in the past."[2] Simmel also depicts reasons why the former members, now converts, feel they must be most dogged in their fidelity to the group of strangers to whose lures they have succumbed. They often then become zealots.[3]

We have already cited Max Scheler to the effect that this renegade has to show fealty to the newly chosen group, defend what it represents, and "engage in a continuous chain of acts of revenge on his spiritual past." Thus some far-left survivors of rebellions in France or the United States as of 1968 later became far-right zealots, and gave vent to their emotions in acts of at least rhetorical vengeance. The Jew who becomes a "born again" Christian may spend her next Christmas visit "home" swinging widely and wildly in her attacks against the Judaism of her family, since she must show how those close to her have failed her.

On this spiritual landscape it is valuable to make distinctions between heretics and renegades in their appearances as strangers. The heretic is someone who consorts with strangers and becomes one. When children of lightly observing Reform Jewish parents choose ultra-Orthodoxy or when children of liberal Protestant parents convert to fundamentalism, as Lewis A. Coser observes them, they can represent either of two different kinds of threats.

> It is less dangerous for a group if the one who breaks with it goes over to the enemy than if, as a heretic, he forms his own rival group (hence the attempt to brand as "agents of the enemy" former group members who have left in dissension). The heretic continues to compete for the loyalty of the members of his former group even after he has left it. The renegade will fight them, the heretic will proselytize. Moreover, by professing to share the values of the group, the heretic creates confusion and hence his actions are perceived as an attempt to break down the boundaries.[4]

The obverse side of this power to repel the majority in the host culture appears in the potential of the stranger to attract. Students of Christian mission have shown how overcoming pluralistic ignorance can blunt impulses to seek converts. Typically, in the nineteenth century it was relatively easy to gain support for British or American Protestant missionaries sent to convert the bad Buddhists of Burma. Such Buddhists were seen as bad because they had imprisoned and caused to suffer some of the pioneer missionaries, whose agencies or teams in turn used the stories of victims to describe Buddhism. Well and good, or well and bad, depending on how one views the missionary enterprise. Those who embrace the pluralist experience can find that for some it dulls the impulse to convert the stranger. While it may be easy to back missionaries to the bad Buddhists, how should people account for and relate to the good Buddhists who live next door? What if their impressive way of life shames the bad Christians who live next door?

Belongers often see strangers who are at home in a pluralist setting as dangers because their presence and activities may cause believers of one sort or another to doubt the integrity of their own commitment. Something in their own faith may have been described to a young person as being superior, exclusive, even uniquely capable of producing positive values. Then, while maturing in a pluralist environment, such persons open their eyes and determine to their own satisfaction that on several levels the faith of others seems superior for the ways it generates better values. The question that naturally follows then is, shall we trust those who handed on and taught us our faith and produced our existing community? Should we at least waver in our own commitment enough to relax in religious observance?

A university campus is an excellent laboratory for anyone who wishes to observe this phenomenon in action. A student arrives at one of them having been schooled in a congenial religious tradition, and having observed its practices into adolescence. Thereupon the random assignment of roommates, extra-curricular activities advertised on campus bulletin boards, and offerings in Comparative Religion courses, expose this person to formerly exotic and esoteric religious offerings. They soon promise to deliver more than could the old-home faith. Confusion or conversion results.

The anti-pluralist therefore reasons: cannot we simply avoid all these problems by ruling the strangers out? Let the cultural majority rule. Pass legislation or seek court rulings that will prevent their arriving or inhibit their action upon arrival. Shelter especially the young, so they can have transmitted to them in isolation the faith and culture of their fathers and mothers. The fear of the other dominates. So those who express such fears must take revenge by portraying the stranger in negative terms and by placing boundaries around her, in order to keep one's own community intact and productive.

Another repelling feature of the strangers' faiths and communities in the eyes of many is that in the pluralist market the advertising of rich and bewildering options makes it hard to make and hold to a commitment. Robert J. Lifton discerned especially that young people lose the boundaries of self and community when faced by a confusing

and seemingly endless set of options and lures. To apply this perception to the religious realm, picture such persons being barraged by
testimonies of celebrities on television to the New Religious Movement of their choice. They then walk the streets and confront
immigrants who embody alien religions just as they speak different
languages. Next, they are invited by notices on the bulletin board to
participate in one or more of the sixty "spiritual" alternatives there
offered, before going on to a movie whose plot further erodes the
boundaries of faith and community. In a single metaphor, picture
such a person walking down a cafeteria line of philosophical and
religious offerings, each more glamorous than the other, or at least
more colorful than the old-time religion back home.

Lifton calls the person in this culture "Protean man":

> I have evolved a concept of "Protean man" – named, of course, after
> that intriguing figure of Greek mythology renowned for his shape-
> shifting – in order to describe an emerging psychological style which
> I believe is characteristic of much of contemporary life . . .
>
> [There is a] break in the sense of connection men have long
> felt with vital and nourishing symbols of their cultural traditions –
> symbols revolving around family, idea systems, religions, and the life
> cycle in general. In our contemporary world, one perceives these
> traditional symbols as irrelevant, burdensome, or even inactivating,
> and yet one cannot avoid carrying them within, or having one's self-
> process profoundly affected by them.
>
> . . . [As for postmodern mass communications – here think of
> religious symbolic transmission:] The images they convey cross over
> all boundaries, local and national, and permit each individual every-
> where to be touched by everything, but at the same time often cause
> him to be overwhelmed by superficial messages and undigested
> cultural elements, by headlines and by endless partial alternatives in
> every sphere of life. In other words, as an individual one can main-
> tain no clear boundaries.[5]

Lifton introduces a note that demands further development: mass
communications as much as the market work against the endeavors

of anyone effectively to screen out the images and lures that come with pluralism, and also in religion.

A corollary of the lure of this potpourri of spiritual options that comes with pluralism is this: the Protean person becomes free to dabble without making commitments, to sample without deciding on a cuisine, to receive some momentary and superficial benefits of the strangers' religions without going through the disciplines that each and any of them demand. If only such pluralist presences would disappear or be blocked and inhibited, says the anti-pluralist, all would be well and the members of the host culture would have time to nurture their young in serious ways.

Lifton's discernment of the emergence of the Protean style in complex societies is matched by another description that he offers. This one goes far toward accounting for the many militant enclave cultures and fundamentalist-minded persons that thrive today. The opposite of the Protean style is constrictive, "the closing off of identity, the constriction of self-process, to a straight-and-narrow specialization in psychological as well as in intellectual life, and to reluctance to let in any extraneous influence." The constrictive is "an essentially reactive or compensatory style." Its partisans work to pass laws, block signals, and even eliminate the presence of the stranger who symbolizes values that come from beyond the group.

Religious bodies act in ways that reflect the impact of the pluralist environment on their theology and decisions. Thus the Southern Baptist Convention, the largest Protestant body in the United States, saw no need to pass constrictive definitions of the role of women for 150 years, until 1998. Then it drew upon some passages in the Bible that not many of them had construed as fervent calls for female submission to males. So long as Baptists did their own interpreting of the Bible, protected as they were on their "home" cultural ground, it was not necessary to render it into virtual dogma and an informal set of interpretations. Of course, biblical texts prescribing female submission had been available. But the strenuous argument for female submission awaited the United States entering a war at a time when

105

the status of women in religions was in question. The acts of sub-mission may have belonged in the category of cultural *vigencias*, not of church law. But by the time the measure was passed, millions of women in the Convention had entered the workforce beyond the home. There they were more exposed than before to non-Southern Baptists and their subcultures. Some of the signals they received there, including Christian feminist appeals, were alluring to many and, of course, mass media invaded the Baptist space with images of liberated and even dominating women. So the Convention voted to ward off such signals, to further a constrictive style.

Similarly, some encyclicals issuing from the Vatican demonstrate an awareness by the Curia that postmodern Catholicism is exposed to other religions as seldom if ever before. While some of the statements show a generosity of spirit – one thinks of *Nostra Aetate* issuing from the Second Vatican Council, about which more, later – there is also concern about open exposure to the religion of strangers. The American bishops, for instance, have found it neces-sary to warn the faithful against American Protestant fundamentalist apocalypticism and its cultural expressions, which ran counter to Catholic views of the future. Here, it is the fundamentalist who is the stranger and who evokes reaction.

Strategies for Accommodation in Pluralism

One strategy for accommodation by many who have chosen to deal with civil pluralism has been to work for the erosion of boundaries among religious groups. They endeavor to relativize the importance of membership in them by simply making less of groups themselves, or by openly repudiating them and their values. This approach, usually codenamed as the favoring of "spirituality" over against "organized religion" or "institutions," has occasioned attacks on some frequently prominent features of religion, features that can most easily offend. These include devotion to particular scriptural canons, the laws of religious institutions, the favoring of hard-edged definitions of dogma, and insistence on communally monitored patterns of behavior.

Of course, advocacy of such individualized spirituality does not exhaust the repertory of potential responses to pluralism, nor does the form this reactive spirituality has taken even exhaust what spirituality has meant and could mean. Most religions have encouraged spiritual traditions, as evidenced by adjectives connected with the term: "Hindu Spirituality," "Native American Spirituality," "Jesuit Spirituality," or "Jewish Spirituality." What is relatively novel is the phenomenon of spirituality unaccompanied by adjectives; in other words, free-form, postmodern collages or assemblages that reject rootage in traditions and seek no warrants in authoritative texts.

While in theistic religions "God" is the focus, the unanchored and unmoored forms of spirituality inside pluralism make the most of concepts such as *energies* in the universe, *connections* to be made with invisible forces and imaginative insights. Some of these spiritualities soon acquire the character of religions. Their constituents and clients follow certain gurus, patronize special bookstores, communicate over defining websites, train disciples, offer retreats, advertise websites, and form collectives defined enough that, in cultures where it is advisable, they apply for tax-exempt status. When they do, these constructs become communities made up of those who appear as apostates, renegades, or heretics to the communities they would replace. They become one more option made up of competitors, those who create confusion inside the fabric of pluralist society. When they take on the character of numerous New Religious Movements (NRMs), they often have been led by authoritarians, are hierarchical, and choose to keep those strange to them at a distance. In recent decades supporters of highly individualized and eclectic expressions of "spirituality," which take the form of polemics against "organized religion," advertise these as reducing the potential of conflict among "faith communities" precisely because they are *not* communal. Satisfying as these may be to those who adopt them, they have little effect on massive religious collectivities around the globe.

107

A second leveling or balancing intention results in the warm appreciation of the other by those who have belonged. In a sense, they forego the privileges or shrug off the burdens of establishment and take on the character of strangers. Or they regard strangers as equally privileged belongers. Many devoted Hindus or Catholics or Jews and others, not all of them liberal, make it a point to be hospitable. They encourage encounter and interaction. Thus the strangeness of the stranger is at least partly overcome.

A third possibility among those who respond positively to pluralism is for groups of believers to use the presence of the stranger to help them reappraise and enrich their own commitments. In nineteenth-century Germany, pioneers in the study of comparative religion spoke aphoristically: *Wer ein Religion kennt, der kein Religion kennt* – Whoever knows one religion knows no religion. The presence of a second faith or even a number of them helps create a mirror, a hall of mirrors, or a prism with which a community can examine its own commitments, a treasury from which its members can borrow.

As an illustration: for a half-century Christians and Jews have met in conversation in communities, seminaries, forums, and wherever they occupy something of the same place. The two traditions had been estranged for twenty centuries, as Christian majorities had treated the Jewish presence as alien, subversive, and evil. There had, of course, been moments of breakthrough, such as sometimes in the late Middle Ages when Islamic and Jewish cultures were both vital and both shared space with Catholics on the Iberian peninsula. But not until the Second Vatican Council in 1962–5 did Catholicism take major steps to open a door to welcome Jews in Rome. Many Jews opened their own doors, thus encouraging their fellow adherents around the world to change.

As many scholars testify, out of such exchanges have come re-explorations by Jewish scholars. These make possible more appreciative and nuanced portrayals of Yeshua the rabbi, Jesus, than those long fostered. Christian theologians in these conversations have in turn testified to many changes in their thinking, changes they have brought to their seminary students, future priests and pastors, or to ecumenical forums in communities. For instance, they have reappraised their sense of covenant, both where they shared a mutual covenant and where they radically diverged. Both the dispersal and the concentration of Jews as a result of the Holocaust and the birth of Israel further inspired interactions, while reflection on these contributed to the over-coming of some strangeness and to an appreciation of more sectors of pluralist society. They freed leaders in both communities to take up divisive questions such as anti-Semitism or the politics of Israel.

Similarly, al-Qaeda zealots, a radical spin-off from Islam that chooses to act in the name of Islam, began attacking Western and then particularly American sites, as they did on September 11, 2001. Religious majorities in countless American communities since that trauma have faced two main options. They could engage in simple dismissal of and formal negation of their Muslim neighbors locally or globally. Or they could begin the process of understand-ing Islam, making efforts to interpret terrorist action and American reaction, and then build on that mutual understanding. At heart, the Muslim and non-Muslim communities remained distinct and maybe wary, but the doors of many of these to each other were no longer closed.

Years before 2001, unless one lived in a Dearborn, Michigan, in particular French communities, or in some other Western sites that included Muslim enclaves, most non-Muslims did not know much about 6 million Muslim neighbors in both nations. Before 2001, Islam was the faith of that billion people "out there" in Muslimdom, strangers *en bloc* and not known neighbors to the rest of the world. The new encounters between Muslims and Christians began with the appraisal of some leaders and many regular citizens in the mirror held up by the other.

Thus, many non-Muslims, confident that whatever else they knew, they were sure of what a jihad was, gave their own unsym-pathetic definition of it as calling Muslims always and only to "holy war" against the West. They soon began to learn a complex history which had a more reserved place for jihad. As quickly as they heard "jihad!" against them, many militant Muslims, particularly in the

Middle East and Europe, counter-attacked with a shouted "crusade!,"
a phenomenon about which they knew nothing positive, if there
had ever been anything positive, or if they had thought about it at
all. Many of them did. What was in their long memories came to be
a theme in the engagements across the Muslim–non-Muslim line.

Out of this web of interactions came many of the features of
interactive life that we shall discuss later. What came to be a minimal
response grew out of or paralleled John Courtney Murray's description of a republic as people locked together in civil argument. They
are "locked together" because they occupy the same place and neither
will leave the neighborhood. That neighborhood today is global. They
are in "argument" because issues that divide stranger from stranger
demand address. At their best, the arguers become "civil." They
prefer the vigorous style that Murray described, to the lethal one
that in the new millennium usually characterizes intergroup reactions.

Citizens in a pluralistic setting have to face up to some measure
of competition among contradictory intense values that they hold
within themselves. Let me illustrate from my own commitments.
Within the Christian world I have identified with the ecumenical
efforts stimulated during the century past. This identification calls
forth a theologically grounded approach to the four marks of the
Christian church: that it be not only holy, catholic, and apostolic, but
that it also be *one*. Its members are to recognize the degree of unity
that is latent in any circumstance and do what they can to remove
barriers to its development. While not looking for or even hunger-
ing for a merger of the separate denominations, I am in the camp of
those who cheer the knocking down of gates and walls around
the sacraments, especially the place called "The Lord's Table," "The
Lord's Supper," the Mass, the Eucharist, or Holy Communion. When
Christians of various communions recognize and invite each other
to this central mystery and observance, "oneness" becomes visible
and tangible as they participate.

On the other hand, I am in the company of Madisonians, that
is, of celebrators of themes proposed and fought for by James
Madison, whom we met here as a major drafter of the United States

Constitution, the Virginia Bill for Religious Freedom, and the First Amendment. Here is Madison's attempt in *The Federalist* to locate the place of pluralism. He wrote this in a context in which he was showing how a republic could limit what he called the "mischief" that factions could work. But he was ironically and probably unwittingly contributing to a rationale for them:

> [From *Federalist* No. 10:] By a faction, I understand a number of citizens, whether amounting to a majority or minority of the whole, who are united and actuated by some common impulse of passion, or of interest, adverse to the rights of other citizens, or to the permanent and aggregate interests of the community. [In other words, the belongers.]
>
> . . . A religious sect [now: "strangers"] may degenerate into a political faction in a part of the Confederacy; but the variety of sects dispersed over the entire face of it must secure the national councils from any danger from that source.
>
> [From *Federalist* No. 51:] In a free government the security for civil rights must be the same as for religious rights. It consists in the one case in the multiplicity of interests, and in the other in the multiplicity of sects.
>
> . . . In the extended republic of the United States, and among the great variety of interests, parties, and sects which it embraces, a coalition of a majority of the whole society could seldom take place on any other principles than those of justice and the general good.[6]

While attending the third session of the Second Vatican Council (1964) I would often converse with Joseph Lichten, a head of the invited American Jewish visitors' group. Over coffee along the Via della Conciliazione he regularly pressed me: how can one promote the unity of Christianity, which commands some degree of loyalty among four-fifths of the American people, and at the same time advocate extension of James Madison's celebration of multiplicity? These appear to be in some contradiction to anyone who is philosophically neat. I could see why Lichten was puzzled, and have to confess that dealing with both realities leaves me uneasy at times.

In politics and practice, however, a different, messier but more productive reading than his is possible. First, there was no danger, or no hope, that separated Christians would come together enough that they would no longer be contributors to that multiplicity. And if they did come together as much as Lichten supposed we wished, the prophetic and self-critical faculty of Christians would kick in, and Christianity thereafter would fragment again. At the same time, I pointed out that the form of the current ecumenical movement was itself recognizing the value of the internal diversity within Christendom and encouraging many expressions of multiplicity in a world of diverse faiths.

This doubleness will mean that believers must work for the common good beyond the interests of their individual tribes, beyond the collectives that tempt them to make strangers of others within the church. Thus, in liberal cultures, those who celebrate pluralism and seek common ground often grow inattentive to their own tradition. In the process, those with exclusivist impulses often find it easy to claim that they are the true representatives of such whole traditions. For instance, in matters of ethical decisions, it is easy to parade a whole encyclopedia of competitive nuances and contentions that one after another Christian group holds in particular, often against other groups. Yet the company of believers is not in so much disarray that its ethical leaders cannot also draw upon a relatively coherent body of moral discourse, at least sufficient to start better arguments than one usually hears.

Doing such, of course, will not settle all the differences: intratribal aggression, as we noted, can often be most fierce. What the act of converging on these resources does confirm, however, is that pluralist societies are not and do not have to be simply chaotic, unable to engage in moral inquiry and common action.

Similarly, the larger company of those who have feared the stranger can take courage from the record of practical situations and circumstances which can minimize the damage of extreme factionalism or the threat that particular strangers, or strangers in company with each other, might represent. Among the counter-forces are the following.

There is a reservoir of public good will. Not all republics are completely Hobbesian, which means that not all individuals and all forces are hostile to or suspicious of each other. They can experience and exemplify mutual affection, which in this context means nothing sentimental. It results from the affective life that is generated by people who have suffered together, found common cause, and known good moments together. Polls taken in most nations reveal that there are such reservoirs of affection and commonality, and that conflict among belongers and strangers is often overstated.

Curiously, secularization, seen at best ambiguously and often as an explicit threat to religious groups, can play a part in dulling the edges of hostile moves among the faiths. It is admittedly hard for those who advance a specific faith to recognize the value of religious indifferentism, but in many contexts secularization, which often brings with it religious indifference, deserves positive attention. If every religious group in a society is at all times and on all fronts and points eager in intense ways to stress its difference from every other, the risks are high that belongers and strangers alike will face or create cultural disaster. The fact that not all care to stress differences and suspicions all the time can be salutary.

Social mobility, an agent of pluralism, is also a potential softener of the abrasive edges where group meets group. So long as the belongers stay fixed in one place and either through pluralistic ignorance or steadfast distancing from others remain isolated and self-defensive, they cannot entertain a positive appraisal of the values of other groups or learn from them. In the contemporary world immigrants, refugees, transferred employees, students, travelers, adventurers, and entrepreneurs pick up stakes and, as individuals or groups, move to new places. Their movement itself becomes an agent in reducing the potential for conflict among the company of those who are immobile and who lack a clear vision of others, whom those fixed in place can easily misunderstand and misrepresent.

Practical necessity, often economically dictated, is also a factor. I have always seen New Netherlands, later New York, to be a pioneer among the thirteen American colonies in advancing eventual religious freedom, and doing so in many more ways than have colonies which usually receive credit. They did this in part for economic reasons. In colonial New Netherlands, the governor, Peter Stuyvesant, wanted to perpetuate the Dutch pattern. This would have meant establishing the Reformed Church, giving it privilege, and thereupon banning or harassing others. He had to give in and acknowledge diversity, however, which meant allowing for pluralist presence. He did so never on ideological or theological grounds, but for purely practical reasons – to compete with other colonies. In numbers of these, strangers in the person of sailors, merchants, and varieties of settlers, could freely come and go. As the newcomers settled in they brought their differences, be these of Protestant, Catholic, or even Jewish lineages. Oliver Cromwell said that the Dutch loved guilders more than godliness. Some of their concern for guilders, their zest for markets, led them to move toward accepting religious pluralism. They did this without evident lessening of religious interest among the religious.

Exogamy, a finally unpreventable practice in a republic, reduces the distance among strangers and belongers. No matter how much parents and leaders in the various religious groups try to keep intermarriage from occurring, it does happen, and often with considerable frequency. While every such familial merger can provoke hostility among families that want to be hostile, they also can work to force them to cooperate and be empathic. While such marriage begins as a one-on-one affair between individuals or among families, the cultural impact of each marriage as their numbers grow is enormous. In Mexico, where the conquerors from Europe cohabited and intermarried with the native peoples, though much of the colonial and national story is sad, it differs from that in the United States. There, despite a large number of unsanctioned exceptions, the whites worked to stay "pure." The fate of the native peoples who survived was to be sequestered on reservations. In the intentions of their conquerors, this meant that they were to be perpetual strangers.

In public education, while young people – or in the case of universities, not so young people – may often bring group animosities to academies, overall the public schools have been places where children of religiously differentiated people interact, usually if not easily, to benign effect.

The surrender of complete autonomy of one religious group coupled with efforts to affirm something of the others has often occurred on the highest levels of authority. When Roman Catholic immigrants in large parishes wanted to cling to Old World languages, archbishops on occasion would insist that English be the language in parochial schools. In the culture of the parishes, however, European ethnic backgrounds survived in theatricals, dances, entertainments, and cuisine. How one relates to the stranger in a society of strangers, which means in a truly pluralistic society, is an issue of practical consequence. The complex field of health and medicine illustrates this. In American society after the middle of the twentieth century the subject of medical ethics became urgent and attractive. It was urgent because of the sudden advances in medical technology and the burden of dealing with governmental, medical, academic, and religious institutions. It was attractive because it held the possibility for caregivers to deal in better ways with a new situation. There was pressure on clinics, hospitals, and hospices to make provision for ethical reflection and counsel under the auspices of such institutions. Fear of malpractice suits, the need to comply with laws, and response to calls of conscience and for humane treatment of patients made the topic attractive. Many of the calls for ethical reflection and advice came from the caregivers themselves, since they experienced stress as they dealt with medical events associated with birth, death, and disability.

Once upon a time the setting up of ethics panels in institutions could have been fairly simple. While most Catholic, Lutheran, Methodist, or Jewish hospitals had served the general public, especially after governmental funding gave most of them little choice, a half-century ago each was still relatively autonomous in matters of ethical policy. That is, in a Catholic hospital, run by a Catholic order of sisters, under a Catholic board of control and with Catholics in key positions on medical and administrative staffs, the leadership only needed to consult the formal teachings of the Catholic Church,

115

especially as these bore on issues of healthcare. They could and must consult and adhere to codes developed by the various associations which brought Catholic medical institutions together. Something similar would go on in a Lutheran, Jewish, or Mennonite healthcare institution.

No longer. The reasonably more open access to clinical care developed since then meant that hitherto distant constituencies were drawn close. The Catholic hospital was soon confronted by the interests of Muslim, Roma, or Jewish staff, patients, their families, and their religious leadership. As the government became ever more involved, even the most religiously defined healthcare institutions had to meet governmental standards and produce new kinds of legal reports, and they found themselves dependent on commercial interests that paid no mind to matters of faith.

Many of these hospitals consolidated their interests with others, often with institutions that did not share their faith. Inevitably, they experienced some dissipation of denominational energies, some lessening of ties to monitors. True, Catholic hospitals could more or less hold their own insisting on specific policies, including, most notably, those relating to abortion and euthanasia. Most hospitals and clinics do not have such precise stipulations, but they may try to follow religious guidelines. I have worked with the Advocate Health Care system, which relates to the Evangelical Lutheran Church in America and the United Church of Christ. The first of these is seen as being in the moderate mainline, while the other is liberal. Panels of both these denominations on occasion interpret and apply their teachings. At times, spokespersons for Advocate have drawn on these and found them very helpful. But the use of these guidelines tends to be unobtrusive, and most patients would not be aware of them. To be honest, many on the staff would also not be conscious of them except when forced to consult them in times of controversy over policies and ethical decisions.

All that being the case, it is natural to ask: who are the norm-setters who are at home in both public and private, tax-based or for-profit and non-profit institutions, that claim no religious tie? And what ethos, what "qualities," of a community, to use Simmel's term, would the host institution draw upon for ethical resources, just as the older kind of hospitals drew on? What about religion in these ethical sources?

The answer would be: on the European continent, in the British Isles and North America, a version of secular rationality, born under Enlightenment influence and nurtured through modernity, would prevail. Law professor and philosopher Kent Greenawalt attempts to define "publicly accessible reasons" for making specific ethical and political decisions.[7] He shows how the most regular proposal for medical (and political) decisions is rationalistic in two dimensions: "in its confidence that reason can settle the merits of competing comprehensive systems and in its claim that the best of systems should be followed in preference to contrasting intuitions." That would mean that proponents of specific theological claims made by families of Amish or Orthodox Jewish patients would normally have to yield to the articulators of a generic and blanketing "rationalist" system.

Greenawalt immediately went ahead with a critique of this proposal, revealing as he did deep skepticism that "publicly accessible reasons really are capable of adjudicating" between numbers of plausible approaches to morality, any more than any of these alone could do. In his reading, the most intelligent philosophers who come up with "comprehensive moral theories" have great difficulty bringing them to bear on specific situations. He found it "unreasonable to suppose that people should eschew all their religious convictions" to make, in his case, political decisions, and in mine at this point, in medical and ethical dilemmas. To ask devout believers to pluck out and throw away their religious convictions would be to ask them to "start from scratch," and this they cannot do.

Greenawalt focused on the proposal of the most influential political philosopher in America, John Rawls, and his antecedents, among them Louis Henkin.[8] Greenawalt writes:

117

> The domain of government, it is suggested, is that in which social problems are resolved by rational social processes, in which men can reason together, can examine problems and propose solutions capable of objective proof or persuasion, subject to objective scrutiny by courts and electors.

Over against this prevalent if not normative view, Greenawalt quotes philosopher Basil Mitchell, who linked Henkin to other liberals. They presume that religion is a private matter that "belongs to the realm of ideals, not to that of interests. It follows that religious considerations, as they affect morality, should have no place in law making."[9]

John Rawls through most of his career also assumed that religious argument, being based on divine revelation, could have no bearing on political and, here applied, on medical–ethical decisions. The contenders on any major front, whatever their private beliefs, put on the garb of being almost nothing but secular, rational, scientific beings in heart and at base. "What is inappropriate is reliance on religious grounds to decide political issues within a society that accepts Rawls's conception of justice." Greenawalt, however, shows that the choice of this approach is not metaphysically non-committal. It is grounded in specific views of the human person in society. So we are free to ask whether Rawls's approach is simply conclusive and all-inclusive. Greenawalt answers no, and then provides a most credible accounting of how religiously committed people exist in modern republics where, in theory at least, government may neither by coercion or persuasion impose a single metaphysical or theological cast on diverse publics.[10]

The secular rational approach is basically what is taught – many would say what *must* be taught – in medical schools that are reflective of the secular society of which they are a part. They deal with a quadrilateral set of topics for reasoning about ethics. These are autonomy, justice, and, reflecting the ancient Hippocratic oath, non-maleficence and beneficence. For planning programs and determining institutional priorities, these four, in the context of expert reasoning, have helped clarify ethical discourse. But they and Rawls's approach have little to tell a family which is deciding whether to "pull the plug" on a senior brain-dead relative.

At such points, families will also draw on their most profound and shaping ethical resources, which often relate to commitments that individuals and groups have made in philosophy and practice, as in their religious communities. For such the questions will begin with "why be just?" That interest does not proceed simply from the philosophical preferences of one generation. What is the status of the "autonomous individual" in the case of someone who believes that humans are made in the image of God and must be committed to life in human community? What do beneficence and non-maleficence mean among people who claim that their only norm is divine law?

A professor of medical ethics at a major medical school has noted that in no crisis situation that he knew of did a family in distress call upon the university to deliver, for example, one Kantian, one Deweyite, one pragmatist or utilitarian, and one rational choice theorist. They call upon and ask for what their rabbi or priest or minister thinks and what their good books say to their community. They may ask what does their good doctor or nurse or administrator, their pastor or mother, think in this situation. In other words, they draw upon themes from revelation, mystery, memory, tradition, community, and hope. The roots of each of these in one tradition may not be the roots of choice for someone from another. Very often several such traditions may have a bearing on ethical choice. Thus, when traditionalist Muslims enter a high-tech American clinic, they will interpret and profess themes that would not come up in some other way and would discomfort the Catholics who operate the hospital.

It would give a false impression were one to take from this survey the sense that all patients or clients are members of religious groups, or that those who are, are well-informed about them. Many may be relaxed, apathetic, amnesiac, and ill-informed about their faith traditions. Life in a contentious pluralist society, however, is causing more of them to become alert to these resources and their limits.

119

They read of or see images of articulate and sometimes extremist members of the traditions dredging up features of each that are embarrassing to many within and scandalous to many outside of such communities. They thereupon have to make their own assessments. The religious bodies of which many are a part may formulate positions and ask members to influence legislation and medical practice. In the society of strangers they are more likely to hear from neighbors, co-workers, or fellow patients both some questions and alternative answers to those questions, and they have to reappraise their own understandings.

In the process they may find that somehow a consensus has emerged, based indeed on secular rationality, the four main themes of current ethical philosophy, the Enlightenment, "the Judeo-Christian tradition," and some other influences. They also may be poised to question whether there ever was a true consensus or whether favored and in-power groups established rules for everyone else. They become involved in probing and argument within their own religious community, and further question the stability or even the existence of a consensus they would have chosen.

Then they face a practical situation. A Seventh–Day Adventist in a public hospital is brain dead. His pastor at the head of the bed and his family have determined that he is ready for heaven and thus for death. Let it happen. At the foot of the bed is an Orthodox Jewish physician who reflects a philosophy fused out of Orthodoxy and the ancient Hippocratic oath: here is life, and we must not tamper. At the patient's side is a Roman Catholic chaplain who did a doctorate in theology and ethics at a major divinity school. The four provide a snapshot of a pluralistic society in action where it counts. Where there is conflict among them, who will win? Will the patient end the conversation by dying, or will an argument and deliberation ensue? Given all this, what will happen? The will of the family and the pastor may well prevail, leaving other parties somewhat troubled, but religious and medical leaders often yield to the family, which has to live with the decision it has advocated before the ethics panel.

What or who will win? Death, as just noticed? Or thoughtlessness, which means that no one takes the initiative to render the matter ethical and worthy of deliberation? Power, in the hands of the institution that represents the larger society's not always well-questioned framework for making decision? Some responses:

1 The clusters of strangers represented by the family and other agents of decision will *not* satisfyingly "solve" all ethical dilemmas. There may be no satisfying solution, no arbiter to decide whether the proper decision was made.
2 It is not likely that one of the many agents representing the "secular rational" approach of Henkin and Rawls will simply lose out to particularists – or, should I say, to "other particularists." So in that instance, why talk?

In many documentable cases, what does win out when the faiths of strangers is represented is what I call a "thickening" of the discourse. It will not produce anything so neat as a straight-arrow secular rational approach. It will eventuate in a thicket, a bramble, of entangled and sometimes not completely unentangleable strands, mixed with branches of other growths. But it is likely to reflect not only the messiness of a pluralist society but also repositories of options that would not have been contemplated in the world of the Rawlsians. The larger society will have benefited because legitimate voices of particularity and often dissent have been heard, and medical care can improve. And the patient or, in life-and-death circumstances that turn to death, the surviving family, will be more at peace, knowing that their moral and ethical concerns have been taken into consideration.

If any positives are going to appear, more and more of the concerned parties have to be open to conversation, and to listen to what strangers, other strangers, are saying, and why they say it. As a result, those who formulate policy will more readily take into consideration these insights and concerns and qualities. Often, otherwise unrepresented voices and parties will be heard.

121

What I have just outlined is not a complete argument against or an attempt to devastate the "Enlightenment project" and one of its heirs, the "secular rationalist" approach to medical ethics. These are on the receiving end of many pot-shots by polemicists who do not take into account the many benefits and assets that have come to republics as a result. They have served to lessen futile expressions of religious controversy, and they do represent values that can be and often are widely shared within and also in a criss-crossing of religious groups.

Those who employ this framework need not settle for monopoly or hegemony to the consensus builders who live under Enlightenment and rationalist influences, but to see them as voices among many. For the time being they may even be privileged because their matrix can serve to help coordinate others and because it aspires to be accessible to the largest number.

Postscript

It may sound as if all the groups and all the religions are in simple and total opposition to each other. Not at all. It is easy to overdo the conflicts, to make too much of the hard cases in which religious groups sound extreme and unyielding. In practice it will be found that they share many interests with the presumed consensus builders and with each other. They often desire similar yields and outcomes. They may come to similar points on different grounds. There is not simple chaos out there. There is, however, complex chaos that needs addressing.

What some speak of as "natural law" undergirding society is not in its content at all points different from what most religions most of the time profess. New levels of consensus and bases for action may emerge on many but, of course, never on all of them. Clinic professionals often act on the basis of the relatively promising points of agreement, leaving them to deal more collegially with the more troubling, more controverted issues.

Advocacy of conversation does not always produce positive results. Learning limits of conversation *within* pluralism is essential. Awareness of this can come from a story to be cherished, even though scholars have successfully challenged its provenance as having come from the quill of St. Benedict. Benedictines often like to quote it for its good-humored or ironic approach to the limits of efforts at civility. The Rule of St. Benedict commits the monks to be hospitable: "Let all guests be received as Christ." Here follows a gloss, once believed to be medieval, on that Rule, an elaboration rich in applicability to contemporary situations:

> If any pilgrim monk come from distant parts, if with wish as a guest to dwell in the monastery, and will be content with the customs which he finds in the place and do not perchance by his lavishness disturb the monastery, but is simply content with what he finds he shall be received, for as long a time as he desires. If, indeed, he find fault with anything, or expose it, reasonably, and with the humility of Charity, the Abbot shall discuss it prudently, lest perchance God had sent him for this very thing. But if he have been found gossipy and contumacious in the time of his sojourn as a guest, not only ought he not be joined to the body of the monastery, but also it shall be said to him, honestly, that he must depart. If he does not go, let two stout monks, in the name of God, explain the matter to him.[11]

All the good will in the world will not bring concord in many cases. Yet, in a world of prejudice and civil chaos, of war and terrorism, efforts to understand what happens when faiths collide can be the first step in minimizing the damage. The invention and practice of pluralism are a necessary but not sufficient part of the address to the situation, and to one such we will next turn.

6

The Risk of Hospitality

When faiths collide, the first counsel they receive from conciliators is that they practice tolerance, that they tolerate each other, that they promote toleration. It cannot have passed the notice of readers that most of the two-score times such words have appeared in this book, I have not shown much enthusiasm for them. In history, yes: the story of the hard-won battles to see tolerance develop in legal or personal life merits exuberant attention. In contemporary affairs, however, investment in toleration has to be cautious and devotion to its promise quite reserved. The opposites of each, intolerance, not tolerating, or non-toleration, of course, will issue in destruction of the sort that collisions of faith communities have wrought. This manifesto advocates not the settling for tolerance but the aggressive risk of hospitality and the consequences that can follow upon the taking of the risk. Hospitality and inhospitableness as a polarity also makes for a better fit in our basic polarity between the religiously formed community of belongers and the religious challenge they see in strangers.

One of the problems with tolerance within pluralism is that those who tolerate often have the power or the will to remake "the other" into some manageable image. Hospitality permits – indeed, it insists on – regarding the other as being really different. My colleague David Tracy, though he writes extensively on theologies of pluralism, has long issued warnings against the softening of pluralism, something to which the idea of tolerating well fits.

The official pluralist too often finds ways to reduce real otherness and genuine differences to some homogenized sense of what we (who is this "we"?) already know . . . some pluralists, the vaunted defenders of difference, can become the great reductionists – reducing differences to mere similarity, reducing otherness to the same, and reducing plurality to my community of right-thinking competent critics. In this light, there is truth in Simone de Beauvoir's bitter charge that "pluralism is the perfect ideology for the bourgeois mind."[1]

It is over against such reducing of otherness through mechanical approaches to pluralism and tolerance that many particularists today rebel. Frustrated at the low yield of endeavors to shift the accent from faith to pluralism, some would abandon pluralism entirely. Sometimes they do this in defense of militant particularities, sometimes because they see it as a shallow time-wasting venture. I once participated in a discussion of university chaplains of many faiths. When I had finished, an Orthodox Jewish rabbi from a major university, known for being both provocative and provoking, shouted: "This is all beside the point. I don't give a s— about pluralism. I just want to help my students see the face of God." His intentions as chaplain for the latter may exhaust all his energies, and it may satisfy the self-centered quest of individuals. But that mission in isolation is an obsolete luxury in a world where those who have seen the face of God through their faith, then want to demean, suppress, or kill those who have seen other faiths or in other ways.

The Rights of Belonging

Those who claim rights of belonging may not in fact formally adhere to a particular religious group, and may not have made and kept a profound commitment to one. When social scientists take polls they often ask, not whether interviewees "belong," but whether they "prefer" this or that faith. "What is your religious preference?" implies a weaker attachment than does the question: "To what religious group do you belong?" Yet those who merely prefer one community of faith over another have usually come to be so at home with the values and qualities of majorities in a particular environment in which they live that they may be made as uneasy as are firm belongers when strangers come along. Typically, many Americans who never practice a faith and who are only dimly aware of its content may be most zealous in defending what they may regard as the tradition of an endangered "Judeo-Christian" nation.

As Simmel put it, groups claim the rights of belonging because they have lived, or thought they have lived, in a place longer than others. These others claim such rights for any number of reasons. Perhaps they have successfully conquered in a revolution, defeated an enemy, been given proprietorship, or on some rationale or other they can claim the rights of belonging. The story of the origins on which they base their claims may mix myth and legend with fact and event. In some cases the separate groups that make up a society or a nation each possess records or live with recent positive memories that confirm their status, at least to their own satisfaction. Somehow, whether by priority, brute exercise of power, or casual preemptive claims, they belong, and they make clear that they know who should not.

Often those who do not want to share space and resources and do not want to be near strangers are counseled not to be prejudiced but to be tolerant. A critique of tolerance for its weak character and the condescension often shown by those who exercise it will follow. For years I have been borrowing a stronger concept from Gabriel Marcel, though the term he uses, "counter-intolerance," is inelegant and hard to communicate. The French Catholic existentialist thinker and dramatist offered his alternative in an essay on tolerance. When tolerance does have a strong base and is a firm expression, he writes, "there is not only the recognition of a fact but of a right, and this recognition can become an act of guarantee."

This should lead us to perceive (and this is paramount) that tolerance is ultimately the negation of a negation, a counter-intolerance; it seems difficult for tolerance to be manifested before intolerance; tolerance is not primitive; it is to action what reflection is to thought.

126

In any case, it is inconceivable without a certain power which sustains it and to which it is, as it were, attached; the more it is tied to a state of weakness, the less it is itself, the less it is tolerance.

Here is how it works out: merely to declare that a polity favors tolerance or that people in a religious group favor tolerating others, means they are pushing up against nothing. There is no muscle in what they profess or do. Someone must come along to test the complacency and serenity of a group or, more strongly, must challenge what it holds dear. The natural instinct then for the tested, the challenged, is to be roused and tempted to be intolerant. It is at this point that counter-intolerance comes into play.

In counter-intolerance, I make use of my awareness of how much my faith, philosophy, and community mean to me. I grow conscious of how delicate and fragile are the holds on faith, how difficult the professing of a philosophy, how important but how tenuous belonging to a community can be. Whoever is reflective about these will find it easier to picture how precarious is the others', the strangers', hold on what they value. I can use my own sense of attachment, telegraphed to the other, as a warrant, a guarantee, that I will not act against them.

Marcel considers what several alternatives to counter-intolerance can mean. If action toward the stranger is based on force or is an effort to proselytize, he writes, this "cannot fail to engender in the other the conviction that I am acting out of self-interest and in order to satisfy my desire to proselytize." Or worse, "that I am a servant of a God of prey whose goal it is to annex and enslave." That would present a "loathsome image of the God whose interpreter I say I am."[2] Expressing counter-intolerance does not mean that there should never be efforts at witnessing, evangelizing, or creating a situation in which conversion can occur. It does alter the character of the approach to any of these.

Searching for a more elegant and easier to communicate term that comes close to being "counter-intolerant," I have found most congenial the counsel to be hospitable, to find philosophical reasons to practice hospitality, and then to act upon them.

A Simple Entrée to the Concept of Hospitality

Since I shall be speaking of the risk of hospitality, I may as well begin by acknowledging that there is risk even in employing and offering the concept of hospitality itself, but it is a risk I am ready to take. In a world where strangers meet strangers with gunfire, barrier walls, spiritually landmined paths, the spirit of revenge, and the record of intransigence, it sounds almost dainty to come on the scene and urge that hospitality has a strong and promising place. There are "hospitality suites" and "hospitality industries" and these suggest something much less strong than the concept and reality of hospitality has meant.

Let me risk even more by beginning with a very intimate and homely parable. Doing so suggests that being hospitable is appropriate in domestic life, but may have nothing to do when faith collides with faith, when belongers have to face strangers. I can only ask readers to remember that, whatever else they are, parables are parables, metaphors are metaphors, figures are figures, on the basis of which it is possible to project larger scenes.

If you are invited to my house and accept, or if you knock on my door and are welcomed, I as a Christian will not remove the crucifix, icons, or other Christian symbolic art from my wall. Out of context and in isolation some of the figures will at least vaguely recall incidents that could irritate people of other faiths, as they may also be disconcerting to many who profess the faith from which the images issue. Some religious feminists may find portraits of Mary suckling Jesus to be offensive. More crucially, the cross, for that matter, has caused and can cause some Christians and many Jews and Muslims to shudder.

The stories behind such symbols, however much in need of interpretation and context they may be, are integral to Christian faith, just as the basic symbols and rituals of others are organically related to other faiths. To obscure the symbols that are both taken for granted in my house and at the same time important to those who live there, will only create confusion or deception. My burden or delight may be to interpret them and not to pretend that they are not part of the history of what draws Christians together and what may push them apart from others.

As I risk hospitality with you, I will not ignore or cancel all observations of the holy seasons, integral to the rhythm of the year and my life as these may be. Of course, if I am thoughtful and self-critical, all along I shall be appraising the meanings, values, and interpretations of the various teachings and symbols. Some would merit questioning within a particular community itself, whether or not a guest is present. I would not place a picture of Abraham on the point of knifing his son Isaac in sacrifice to God on the wall of a ward in a children's hospital or bedroom, and would reserve for other contexts contemplation on what that scene means or could mean.

Self-criticism of a tradition is a key to the practice of hospitality. Housecleaning occurs before the guest is invited and arrives. If I have posted pictures of medieval statuary in which Judaism is identified with swine and the synagogue with blindness, I will have been swinish in my taste and blind in my understanding, anticipated guest or not.

Everything said about hospitality in a home has parallels when one invites strangers to worship, where the symbols and rituals appear with greater frequency, clarity, emphasis, and potential for causing offense.

So much, for the moment, for the domestic Christian case. Conversely, if you invite me on a Friday night to your Jewish home, I do not expect you to hide the symbols or forego the rituals of your house. I will not learn anything and certainly will not learn to know you if you would not light the candles, do not include the mother's prayer, nor recite the ancient blessings that come with Shabat observance. I came, I will say, precisely to learn more of who you are, to what you belong and how you express belonging. Thinking or saying something like, "Because the *goyim*, the Gentiles (the "other" people) are coming, we will not do any of the things that we do other weeks," deprives the stranger of hospitality and enlightenment. Impoverished by the lack of a rich experience of the other being faithful leads the guest to return home in confusion, having found no opportunity to learn from what was typical and what helps explain the host. As with home, so with synagogue or mosque.

The important point is this: during the time that either of us is within the gate or under the roof of the other who is strange to us, much occurs. We greet, eat, gesture, listen, speak differently because of the presence of the other, become sensitive to the changes we must make in our own outlook and community, and emerge as different beings than we were before the possibly tense but often enjoyable experience of mutual hospitality.

Another parable or illustration of hospitality shows how it gets effected on a less domestic, more public stage. The whole modern ecumenical movement for Christians and the movement that brings different faiths into encounter are based on something like it. A bigger house than the parabolic "mine" is the pope's, the Vatican. During the first session of the Second Vatican Council in 1962, Pope John XXIII undertook self-criticism and reform of his own house, both because he had met invited representatives of other faiths and in order to meet more of such strangers on more congenial and familiar terms.

We are told, for example, that the pope was listening to Mass broadcast on Vatican radio in Holy Week. He heard the officiating priest include in his prayers a traditional phrase about "the perfidious Jews." Previous popes, sad to say, may have heard that phrase with different ears and John XXIII may even have voiced it himself in stipulated prayers years before this incident. But this pope had come to know Jews personally, to regard them positively, and while noting the differences, to stress theological similarities or parallels among the believers in both faiths.

When Jews began to accept hospitality in "his" house – the council to which they had been invited as representatives of 15 million Jews – the pope knew enough and had the power to declare that such a prayer about perfidy would never again be heard in the Catholic Church. Of course, informed and well-traveled Jews knew that this prayer was not the only offense to them in Catholicism.

They could, however, recognize the removal of that prayer to be a signal that better times could be ahead. At the council, strangers from other communities, including Orthodox and Protestant fellow Christians, still significantly called *separated* brothers and sisters, experienced change among themselves as they became aware of the repentance, resolve, and new invitations of Roman Catholics.

The Vatican and the council represent controlled environments in which people of power had the freedom to initiate change among themselves and for their bearing toward others. In the civil realm it is more difficult to conceive of change in such terms. A civil society is made up of so many disparate groups that they cannot so easily converge on a single set of texts or authority to effect change, as Catholics could do.

Who decides which religious groups belong as hosts in communities, especially in the public zones of a nation? Often, those who have belonged longer and enjoyed the myth of their past "sameness" see the stranger as a potential violator of the national bond. When citizens sing "God Bless Our Native Land" or, in the United States, "God Bless America," one must ask, who is the God who is invoked? Are some invocations of deity out of bounds because they disrupt harmony? Are some privileged, so that they can exclude the prayers of strangers? Who owns the public space and who determines how its hours of sacred ritual are to be used? Where Christians are in the majority in a nation, they are in a position to engage in self-examination, though they may not do it frequently or in depth. Other faiths in other nations can do the same kind of self-appraising on the basis of their holy books and the traditions that issue from them.

For the 1.8 billion people named Christian around the globe, people for whom the word of the Bible counts for something, the biblical understandings of hospitality are to inform practices. Since these Christians in their various groups are widely dispersed, in most nations of the world they also interact with people of other faiths. Some of these people also affirm the concept of hospitality and may even be more generous in practice of it than are many Christians.

That may be true, but at the moment we will stay with the Christian example, built as it is on that of ancient Israel. Being hospitable, say biblical scholars, meant that a person was open "to receive and show hospitality to a stranger, that is, someone who is not regarded as a member of the extended family or a close friend."[3]

For the Christian case, let scholar Darrell Fasching spell out some of this:

> To welcome the stranger . . . inevitably involves us in a sympathetic passing over into the other's life and stories and a coming back into our own life and stories enriched with new insight. To see life through a story which requires us to welcome the stranger is to be forced to recognize the dignity of the stranger who does not share our story.[4]

Such efforts more often than not can be frustrated. Even on domestic scales, however, the idea of putting biblically based ideas of hospitality into action can be risky in the face of one's own constituency. One out of myriad contemporary examples come from the Episcopal Diocese of New York. It was raising funds for rebuilding a mosque in Afghanistan after the terrorist attack in the United States and American counter moves in Afghanistan.[5] Daniel J. Wakin tells the story of how this effort "to do a good deed in the name of faith" met difficulties in a typical instance. Villagers in an area north of Kabul had complained that the American military damaged the building while battling against the Taliban fighters who had occupied it. Bishop Mark S. Sisk thought that if New Yorkers would help rebuild the mosque, they would be acting out of a sense of Christian duty and in congruence with the "message that pluralism is part of civil society." The bishop was met with hostility by many in his diocese, including David Virtue, publisher of the conservative Episcopal paper *Virtuosity*. "It's about the dumbest thing imaginable," he wrote. Why not help poor African Christians rebuild their churches? "Islam is a religion we are in confrontation with." Sisk responded, mentioning that his diocese had already sent large sums of money to

African Christians. But in this particular case, he reasoned that even if in a just cause Americans had "destroyed the thing," the Christians among them had a special obligation to help rebuild. Complex negotiations within the diocese followed, after which some funds were taken to Afghanistan by a personal representative. Yet the leadership expressed disappointment that not more people had supported the venture. The bishop also expressed regret that he could get no Jewish donors to come forward. Reactions of some Episcopalians and Jews to ventures like this are completely understandable, given bad histories and the terror of September 11, 2001. But biblical injunctions to practice hospitality, thought the bishop, remained to be heard and followed.

A retired bishop of the Episcopal Church, C. Fitzsimons Allison, of South Carolina, also blasted the effort to rebuild a mosque instead of Christian churches. He went on to say he suspected that the liberal New Yorkers were operating out of syncretistic motives, and charged that "being generous to other faiths is discarding the uniqueness of the Christian faith." In reply, Dr. Lucinda Mosher of the diocese's Episcopal–Muslim Relations Committee said that the villagers they helped were themselves victims of Islamic fundamentalists. And, she went on, it was being faithful to God's will for people to be agents of reconciliation. "Christianity teaches unconditional love, and what love could be more unconditional than to build a house of worship for a community other than your own?"

We have to let the New Yorkers and Floridians fight the battle over hospitality and turn to the biblical record which they were remembering or forgetting in disparate ways. Whoever wants to promote hospitality to the stranger in areas of the world that have historically been or presently are influenced by biblical thought may find it startling to see how central was the concept of dealing hospitably with the stranger in any talk about ethics in the worlds of the Old and New Testaments.

When someone asks catechized Christian adults what mutual hospitality means, their impulse is normally to begin by reflecting on what it means to be created in the image of God, for one of the main bearings of God toward humans is to show hospitality. In these scriptures God, surprisingly, is depicted both as the belonger and the stranger, the host and the guest. The main theme of the early biblical history found God guiding Israel out of its alien status to a land that was to belong to them and to which they would belong. The scriptures often picture God as being hospitable. Even the songs in the Psalms reinforce this theme. Psalm 39:12 is basic to the acknowledgment that Israel began as a stranger, a foreigner: "For I am your passing guest, an alien, like all my forebears." It was God's land that became the gift to Israel, which meant that God was hospitable in sharing a place. In Leviticus 25:23 Israel was reminded of the terms at the root of the divine–human transaction: "the land is mine; with me you are but aliens and tenants," so "throughout the land that you hold, you shall provide for the redemption of the land," they were told, so they had to follow prescribed ecological practices. Such a concept, by the way, informs those today who, invoking the biblical tradition, promote environmental policies based on stewardship. They do not "own" the land but they "hold" it in their generation.

For Christians, any talk of hospitality across the boundaries of regions, cultures, and faiths must reflect some understandings of the New Testament background. Fortunately, for what we are stressing, the New Testament Greek incorporates the word for "stranger" into "hospitality." The stranger, alien, *xenos* (Matthew 25:35, 38, 43ff., 27:7; 3 John 5; see Ephesians 2:19, *paroikoi*; Hebrews 11:13; Acts 17:21) appears juxtaposed with an opposite, *xenia*, hospitality, or even the guest room where the guest is lodged (Philemon 22; Acts 28:23, hospitality; Romans 12:13, being hospitable; 1 Peter 4:9; 1 Timothy 3:2; Titus 1:8). The Greek term survives in words like xenophobia, fear or hatred of strangers; xenolith, a fragment of a rock that happens to be included in another rock, as a stranger; xenophile, the love of strangers and foreign things. Any number of biological terms, such as xenobiotic, xenogeneic, and xenotropic, are combinations that point to "foreign" elements in cells, plants, and the like.

Fear of the stranger shows up in words other than those beginning with *xeno*. Thus, the American colloquialism NIMBY ("not in my backyard") reflects the abhorrence by some of that which they regard as alien to a particular ecology and human neighborhood. "There goes the neighborhood," it is said when the stranger, the immigrant, moves in. Groups that have worked for the resettlement of homeless people in middle-class neighborhoods or to provide housing for the mentally retarded or parolees in an area that has not experienced such as neighbors regularly witness the rise of xenophobic fears, fear of the stranger. Most of these cases have little to do with religion, but when religion is part of the experience, everything intensifies.

The biblical examples and commands are ample:

"Extend hospitality to strangers" (Romans 12:35)
"A bishop must be hospitable" (1 Timothy 3:2)
"A widow [must have] shown hospitality" (1 Timothy 5:10)
"Do not neglect to show hospitality to strangers, for by doing that some have entertained angels without knowing it" (Hebrews 13:1–3)
"Be hospitable to one another without complaining" (1 Peter 4:9)

The long passage in Ephesians 2:11–21 makes the showing of hospitality the test of vital faith. Ephesians illustrates the life of a community made up of those who had been hostile strangers as Jews and Christians. By practicing hospitality to each other they had already been made into "one new humanity" (2:15). The author characteristically sought to motivate change among the two formerly alienated camps by recall of the past. The recipients of the letter were to remember that they had been "strangers in the community of Israel, outside God's covenants and the promise that goes with them." But now those who had "once been far off" had been "brought near."

Georg Simmel could have drawn his basic distinctions from such lines. Christ had "broken down the enmity which stood like a

135

dividing wall" between the two peoples. The peak of this came with the pronouncement: "Thus you are no longer aliens in a foreign land, but fellow citizens with God's people, members of God's household." Realizing this new humanity in social circumstances of congregational life was not easy, but a new charter developed for the coexistence and interaction of the two peoples.

In the gospels, Jesus, the model, only "tented" in the world (John 1:10–14), and yet he belonged to it so intimately that when he died his believers interpreted the act as a giving of his life for that world. In the gospel stories, he had no place to lay his head, but was constantly the stranger who had to be welcomed into the homes of hospitable people, poor and rich, acceptable and unacceptable types as they were. In the most famous passage, Matthew 25:31–46, the gospel has him describing himself as the invisible person behind the visible mask and manner of the stranger, the alienated one.

John Koenig has traced the concept of hospitality to the stranger through the New Testament, along the way setting down some signposts for our contemporaries who locate themselves in the biblical tradition. He is brutally realistic:

> Hospitality has its shadow side. Some of us will always be deemed unacceptable, unworthy of entry to the place of company we seek. And we in turn will fail to welcome others when we occupy the post of doorkeeper. Indeed, even when welcoming does happen, we sometimes allow it to degenerate into a trading of polite formalities, or worse, a time of mutual abuse on the part of guests and hosts . . . Competition, prejudice, ostracism – all of these occur with regularity in our attempt to be hospitable.[6]

Incidentally, Koenig also pointed to a linguistic turn that is so threatening to positive biblical approaches to hospitality that it made me entertain the possibility of dropping the term: "Furthermore, particularly in North America and Europe, hospitality has become increasingly a commercial concept . . . And of course prostitution by both sexes continues to offer itself as a kind of parody of the guest–host relationship."

In our world where faiths collide, hospitality brings with it dangers we have already associated with the stranger: it can be both too threatening *and* too alluring. However, we would not have many words left in the vocabulary if we had to drop all terms that have almost accidentally acquired uncongenial connotations. The word hospitality and what it points to are too basic to religious traditions for us to jettison them. Koenig shows the strength of this at once:

> Complementing [New Testament usages] is a tradition inherited from the Greek and Near-Eastern peoples (and well represented in the Hebrew Bible) concerning a sacred bond between guests and hosts. According to this tradition, which has virtually disappeared from contemporary Western culture, hospitality is seen as one of the pillars of morality upon which the universe stands. When guests or hosts violate their obligations to each other, the whole world shakes and retribution follows.

When he wrote this in 1985 Koenig observed that in the United States there had been an increase in suspicion of strangers. As immigrants and refugees arrived in great numbers, they experienced reactions that were often negative. Those were Cold War days when the Soviet-bloc nations and their people represented the strangers about whom citizens of the West understandably had reservations. And "stateless people" in their marginal existence wandered, seeking a place to settle. Along the way, Koenig wrote, "they may indeed constitute threats to what we think of as rights, especially our sense of home." After citing incidents of xenophobia, Koenig returned to "the biblical vision of strangers, that broader vision that counters the risks inherent in hospitality with God's loving embrace of all nations." After September 11, 2001, with the terrorist attack on American towers and powers, there were ever more reasons for citizen majorities to be suspicious of strangers, often including all of Muslim faith in their range of scrutiny.

Koenig, to good effect, quoted the Quaker lay theologian Parker Palmer. In his writings, hospitality offers not only risks but benefits to host and stranger, and means:

inviting the stranger into our private space, whether that be the space of our own home or the space of our personal awareness and concern. And when we do so, some important transformations occur. Our private space is suddenly enlarged; no longer tight and cramped and restricted, but open and expansive and free. And our space may also be illumined . . . Hospitality to the stranger gives us a chance to see our own lives afresh, through different eyes.[7]

Such words may sound so rich in promise that they border on sentimentality and could be heard as an underestimation of the risks that go with hospitality. But Koenig and I here adduce it as a reminder that hospitality remains a measure of human two-way interaction. Christian, Muslim, Jew, Hindu, members of new religious movements, fundamentalists, and liberals who share nationhood often have difficulty coming to even preliminary common agreements about the potentials in citizenship. Clearly, some groundrules have to be worked out to make the urgent risk-taking worthwhile. Koenig's goal is to see that the belonger who shows hospitality and the stranger who receives it become partners. In our world that might mean that they become partners in enlarging the sphere of hospitality among the faiths as they work for peace and justice.

Koenig provides an example of risked hospitality from an incident during World War II. He cites Philip Hallie's account of the citizens of Le Chambon, a French village. They hid Jews who were on the run for their lives from the Nazis. The longtime dwellers in Chambon sheltered Jews in their own homes, at risk of death, or guided them to refuge in Switzerland. Why? From studying their story, Hallie wrote:

I learned that the opposite of cruelty is not simply freedom from the cruel relationship; it is *hospitality* . . . When I asked them why they helped these dangerous guests, they invariably answered, "What do you mean, 'Why?' Where else could they go? How could you turn them away? What is so special about being ready to help (*prete a servir*)? There was nothing else to do." And some of them laughed in amazement when I told them I thought they were "good people."[8]

To project such a background of imagery involving belongers, strangers, and hospitality against the script of today's events is itself full of risk, a call to face dangers. The stranger, often associated with a religious group and its symbolism, may have been far off, but is now brought close through media of communication. Hospitality was rendered more risky because of the potential that the stranger may be equipped with dangerous weaponry. This is a fact that calls for alertness among even those hosts who are informed and moved by biblical injunctions to practice hospitality.

When ancient Israel was told it was the elect people, and after it created solemn assemblies that kept all others at a distance, thereupon neglecting hospitality and blurring perceptions, at least some prophets worked to relativize their absolute visions and commitments. Thus the prophet Amos 9:7:

> Are you not like the Ethiopians to me,
>   O people of Israel? Says the LORD.
> Did I not bring Israel up from the land of Egypt,
>   And the Philistines from Caphtor and the Arameans from Kir?

In the Second Isaiah, the Persian King Cyrus, who had made it possible for Israel to return from exile to Jerusalem, is seen as the stranger at the host's table, but he is granted privileges by being named and hosted by Yahweh, the LORD. Cyrus certainly was a stranger: a captor of Israel, not a worshiper of Yahweh, and perhaps an administrator of bad policy against the people of Israel. But he gets to be called the Messiah, "the Anointed," the shepherd of Yahweh's people, though he did not seek the titles and would not have recognized them had he heard them:

> [Yahweh] says of Cyrus, "He is my shepherd and he shall carry
>   out all my purpose . . .
> Thus says the Lord to his anointed, to Cyrus,
> Whose right hand I have grasped
> To subdue nations before him
> And strip kings of their robes,

To open doors before him –
And the gates shall not be closed . . .
I have aroused Cyrus in righteousness (Isaiah 44:28; 45)

If today the stranger is the new person next door, the immigrant, the refugee, the exile, in the world of the Bible the stranger made an especially strong demand on those who belonged in a particular place. Those who did belong were in range of contacts with friends and relatives who could provide a place of shelter and food. Widows and orphans usually lacked such ties and were seen therefore as newly "estranged." They would not inherit land or possessions.

No one was more vulnerable in any circumstance than strangers, who suffered from cruel climatic conditions, usually of the desert sort. They were vulnerable to wayfaring robbers and murderers. Strangers needed daily supplies of food and even more frequent access to water. The relatively settled people, the nomads with tents who had some claim on a place, always took pains to locate themselves at water sources. To turn away the stranger from them could be equivalent to committing murder.

Another hospitable use of water once a stranger was in the house can be implied from the New Testament story of Jesus washing his disciples' feet (John 13:5–20). This narrative is often interpreted as reflecting an ancient Near Eastern gesture of providing not only comfort for the sojourner, but also humbling one's self. Then the stranger could well conclude that the host was not filled with malicious intent toward him. When the Pharisee Simon (Luke 7:36–47) did *not* greet Jesus with water for foot washing, he was seen to be insulting his guest and expressing malice, even hostility.

Not to offer food was also a hostile gesture, interpreted as such, as in the story told in Judges 8:4–17, when Gideon, in unconscionable acts of vengeance, killed people at Penuel and Succoth because they did not follow canons of hospitality. His was an ironically inhospitable act itself.

If the stranger in Israel was vulnerable, the host often also became so. The sojourners had no laws or police for protection, so the

140

person who took them into his tent or house had to do the protecting. In Judges 19:23 townspeople wanted to harm a guest, and the elderly host had to grovel: "This man has come into my house"; leave him alone.

It is no surprise that, like the earliest Christians pictured in the New Testament, later disciples developed traditions of hospitality. Still later, this was a main feature of communal monasticism. A monk who wanted to be self-reliant was ordinarily not found to be responsibly hospitable. Most monks, however, formed houses in which, as the Benedictine Rule put it, all guests were to be received as Christ. Opening the door to the faith-guest was an act of faith, because the stranger could have malign intent and the ability to follow through on it. Here was risk, again.

Many features of hospitality are not of interest in the present argument. They retain mainly metaphoric value, but on occasion these physical outreaches were and are central to the more philosophical and religious reachings out. Thus the hospitable received the stranger into their tent, a form of lodging that allowed for little security in the face of the potentially murderous or plundering stranger. There was always risk.

Those who study the social background of the people represented in the scriptures of ancient Israel provide important insight for today. In that world where trade was important one could not count on hostels or hotels to satisfy the need for lodging. The disciples of Jesus also were expected to go on a journey taking nothing, which means they had to assume that someone in each place would be hospitable.

Further, in the world of nomads, while no one belongs to the land, they belong to each other. They experience little security except that provided by their closeness to the others in the tribe or clan. Yet, even in such circumstances, the scriptures made clear: the stranger has a right to hospitality, which the host is obliged to provide. If someone comes to attack the stranger, the host is also obliged to defend him as if he were part of the family.

In cities, because there were more options, including inns for travelers and strangers, such hospitality was less in demand. By the

141

time of the Jesus story (Luke 2:7) we hear of such an inn; these were characteristically provided and paid for by the people who used them.

Centuries earlier in Deuteronomy 16:10–14 we can read prescriptions for the Festival of Weeks. These called for offerings and promised blessings in which Israel should "rejoice before the LORD your God – you and your sons and your daughters, your male and female slaves, the Levites resident in your towns, *as well as the strangers, the orphans, and the widows who are among you – at the place that the Lord your God will choose as a dwelling for his name*" (emphasis mine). Once again, they were thus to remember that they had been strangers as slaves in Egypt.

Sometimes there were inconveniencing stipulations. In Exodus 12:48–50, "If an alien who resides with you wants to celebrate the passover to the LORD, all his males shall be circumcised; then he may draw near to celebrate it; he shall be regarded as a native of the land." No uncircumcised person dared eat of it; "there shall be one law for the native and for the alien who resides among you." The result of such a stricture is ambiguous: on one hand, it amounts to the equivalent of conversion in the modern world. On another, it shows how those who belonged dare not make lineal descent from previous belongers the criterion for membership in the group.

The Modern Setting

Those scriptural glimpses belong to societies most of whose details escape us or fail to interest us. But the hospitality there described and honored has a bearing on the way modern people, especially Jews and Christians, relate to their tradition in republics. In such societies, where there can be open discourse among groups, a key signal of hospitality appears when groups begin to regard each other with civility. Of course, it is possible to make a fetish of the concept of being civil, and some may use the quest for civility as a way of trying to evade controversy or to silence the other. Yet there is no way for

142

hospitality to proceed without civility. The uncivil host is regarded as hostile; the uncivil guest is disruptive of the community that should emerge when there is interaction.

Let me report on an effort in which I was involved and which moved far enough along that it belongs in this manifesto. The Park Ridge Center for the Study of Health, Faith, and Ethics for several years before 1998 convened a body of researchers and ethicists from a variety of traditions to pursue "Principles of Religious Civil Discourse." The groups represented included Muslims, Native Americans, Baha'i, Orthodox and Reform Jews, Buddhists, Unitarian Universalists, Roman Catholics, Hindus, representatives of African-American religious bodies, Friends, Mennonites, Evangelicals, and a number of mainline Protestant bodies. Through a number of conferences and by developing a set of case studies, this group formulated principles and gave advice, some of which was condensed into a booklet. Since I was present at almost all the meetings, monitored the research, and was one of three drafters of the document, and because upon rereading it I find it, I hope not immodestly, to represent something of the "state of the art" and personal enough to be part of this manifesto, I will draw on it in the paragraphs ahead.[9]

We began with the premise that what often get called "culture wars" are really, at heart, "religious wars." This appears to be ironic, since all the faiths just mentioned define themselves as seekers of reconciliation, promoters of love, spirited by *shalom*. In many communities, religious participants are excluded when citizens deal with basic issues because the moment these reconcilers-by-reputation speak up, they heat up debate and often lead to its premature termination. Yet, because they have much to say and are important elements in a society, when they are absent, many of the crucial aspects of debate are hidden from view. The outcomes then satisfy neither those who ignored or excluded them nor, of course, those who were the excluded and thus the silenced ones.

For all the problems that have appeared when public discourse includes religious themes, it is also clear that the texts and traditions of faith

143

communities have much to offer by way of including calls for effecting social justice, working toward healing, and provoking profound thought.

On the assumption that conflict, which is inevitable, can be turned creative, the Center joined others who have tried to bring out the positive side of the traditions in their bearing on civil society.

First, participants worked on a set of principles that the Center had found of use when convening and presenting materials for the troubled International Conference on Population and Development at Cairo in 1994. Despite all the efforts by so many to be productive, there had been a meltdown.

. . . People of conviction shocked each other and a watching world as they clashed over some of the most volatile topics of the day: family planning and the nature of the family; the rights of women; gender and sexuality; and abortion and birth control . . . In a setting where profoundly convinced believers speak up, as in Cairo, what can easily occur is intense conflict and communication breakdown, resulting in deep frustration and a legacy of continuing misunderstanding.

Looking ahead to another such conference in 2004, the Center embarked on the six-year effort whose originating proposals I am here incorporating.

Participants wrestled with "The Nature of Civil Discourse in the Public Square." The principles here sound commonsensical, but they are in practice hard to follow. First, "welcome the diversity of beliefs and opinions." Suppressing or ignoring voices breeds resentment and narrows the range of ideas. Next, "recognize civil discourse as a process," not a product. On any basic issue it is unrealistic to picture complete settlement among groups in controversy. What we are talking about is not like labor–management conflicts and meetings, out of which must come new contracts. Here, each outcome leads into a next stage, and all must expect setbacks as much as they hope for advance.

The next one, "realize and teach that profound social issues have religious dimensions," hardly sounds like a necessary reminder in this book, wholly devoted as it is to that theme. But this realization is rare at the table where divisive issues in communities come to the fore.

The most nearly utopian of the principles in the report advises: "Understand that religious belief frequently calls for some form of civil discourse." Creating a climate in which the stranger gets a hearing does not mean that all potential participants will want to take part. Some religious groups fear that even showing up suggests an affirmation of beliefs and groups they have determined are heretical and destructive. Still, the movement toward civil discourse often does bring new people to the conversation.

A second major part of the principles, here applicable to the situation of hospitality to the stranger or among strangers, is called "Covenants of Conversation." Participants are called to pledge, first, "to act and speak with integrity and to regard others as doing so"; then, "articulately to express their own faith," to "act respectfully in the face of non-religious knowledge because of religious limits," and to "speak to failures and mistakes of one's co-believers."

The last two of those are often difficult to bring forward, since there is often a kind of public relations sense that "we" must make the best possible representation in the face of others. The first involves admitting that non-religious knowledge may supplement or even contradict what we often have cherished, and, second, that we are fallible. As before, it would be naive to expect that all groups will be forthcoming in such settings, but aspiring to improve the situation is better than to ignore it or fall victim to unquestioned misrepresentations.

A third part calls for "Engaging the Other," as strangers meet strangers in the context of what is intended to be a hospitable situation of conferring. First, "make efforts to engage on a personal level." Too often, encounters among faiths involve reports of task forces, formal documents, and statements of position that often appear in hardened form. If estrangement is then to be overcome, an open one-on-one encounter must occur. The counsel is brisk: "tell stories," since stories are often more open-ended than are dogmas, doctrines, creeds, and tenets. Through stories the stranger becomes a person.

145

"Act on the basis of relative and partial agreements." If settlement is impossible and civil discourse is a process, it is still possible to act on the basis of partial clarifications. "Listen to the voices of the previously excluded." And "put words into actions." Some plan of action and some action must follow on the basis of the conversation.

Finally, "Living with Conflict During and After Conversation and Argument" begins with the need to "recognize that conflict is inevitable and can be creative." So "take steps to assure that the conversation moves beyond conflict or stalemate." A tag line that follows asks much: "Inventory the religious resources and bring them forth." Often in such encounters one discovers not only resources among strangers but also overlooked resources in one's own experience and that of one's community.

The Limits of Hospitality in Macro-Conflicts

Even as I processed the words in the preceding paragraphs I almost lost heart. Many a reader will see how futile they seem in the context of collisions between people of faith. Conflict has gone so far that civil discourse remains beyond range. Picture Palestinian Arabs and Jews bringing specifically religious issues to the table as they address their conflicts. They would smile in condescension, then sneer at or trample the pages you have just read. Picture trying to get militant Shi'ite and Wahhabi Sunni Muslims to the table with non-Muslims in any case. For that matter, picture there even being a table! Promoters of conversation and adjudicating among the faiths often are overlooked and unheard before a crisis and then chided because they have no adequate plan or power when situations have exploded. That reality does not let the promoters be relieved of responsibility in future cases.

An illustration: after September 11, 2001, there was no way that, supposing one could find them, leaders of al-Qaeda could be lured to the table with anyone else, quite literally *anyone* else – including other Muslims. At the same time, in countless communities in the

United States and sometimes in Western Europe, there have been genuine efforts by Christians, Jews, and people of no religious identification to set up circumstances in which local Muslims took part, were heard, and helped effect change. Many a team of medical ethicists in clinics or national forums has found ways to let the process lead to progress. While the Muslim down the street in the United States may crave an end to Muslim-inspired hostility 8,000 miles away, she may well already profit in many parts of her life from being understood by a formerly suspicious or hostile neighbor eight doors way.

Interactions of responsible leaders across the boundaries of religions never make news comparable to that of conflict, especially armed conflict. Television cameras rarely converge on a set of scholars or impassioned lay people who surround a table and look each other in the eye as they ponder ways to promote peace. Nearby bombing, war, or terrorist activity, even by tiny minorities of those faiths that are represented in the conference room, attract the cameras and the reporters. Yet advocates of efforts to cross boundaries progress, even if out of the spotlight.

Most activity toward overcoming strangeness will occur away from cameras and reporters. It occurs in local communities, even in individual minds and hearts. To further the cause, it will be of strategic importance that participants not try to settle in advance the most profound metaphysical questions about the religion of the other. They might have to leave open the question asked by Avishai Margalit from the Hebrew University in Jerusalem:

> Can Judaism, Christianity, and Islam be pluralistic? The question is not whether they can tolerate one another, but whether they can accept the idea that the other religions have intrinsic religious value. Christians, said Goethe, want to be accepted, not tolerated. This is presumably true of Jews and Muslims as well. The question is whether each of these groups is willing to accept the others, that is, to ascribe value to the others' life-style, so that, if they have the power, they will not only refrain from persecuting the others but will also encourage the flourishing of their way of life.

Put differently, do the three religions allow their adherents to ascribe intrinsic value to competing religious ways of life? In competing ways of life, beliefs and values essential to one of them contradict beliefs and values essential to the other.[10]

Appropriate answers to his questions will be expected from those who seek to find satisfying philosophical answers to religious questions. These answers will have some bearing on the questions of proselytizing and converting others. How they see each other's contributions will have an influence on ethical questions within pluralist societies. Theologians are busying themselves with efforts to answer them.

However, for what we call civil pluralism, the creative interaction among people who may share *some* religious commitments but not all, whose stories are incommensurable, cannot wait for answers that are finally satisfying to the philosopher. They have to live "in the meantime," seeking civil peace and just societies among those who are different because they came as strangers, and thus as menaces, to each other – but who, by practicing "counter-intolerance" and hospitality, made it possible to minimize conflict and produce works of civil value.

All the alternatives – tyranny, persecution, prejudice, indifference, condescension, and more – are worse. Whether John Courtney Murray was right, that religious pluralism is against the will of God, is not something that has to be settled for civic society to be constituted and to advance. That it is the human condition, and results from the way the cards of history are dealt, is obviously true. That it will not marvelously cease to trouble the human city is likely. In conversation, Father Murray allowed me subversively to relocate the adverb, which makes the end of the sentence sound like a hope: that it will not cease marvelously to trouble the human city.

As individuals, religious bodies, and other institutions practice and reflect on hospitality in both the most intimate and the most public zones of life in society, they can help that hope be realized: a marvel, in a time of destruction.

148

7

Theological Integrity in Response

This book being a manifesto, I should make manifest one of my assumptions. A blend of realism and theological conviction prompts it. As for the realism: the notion that interactions of faith communities would lead to their complete overcoming of differences and toward their merger into one is a utopian notion. We can presume that four or five of the world's six billion people are dug in, entrenched, at ease, with their faith traditions or their secular commitments, unmovable, not shopping for change. They are unready to be swallowed up or dissolved at the expense of everything they consider to be redemptive or fair. As for the theological conviction: the notion that interactions of faith communities should lead to their complete overcoming of differences and toward their merger into one violates the commitments of faith communities and the stories that animate them. They cannot and will not give them up.

Those words are not intended to be dismissive of the work of creative organizations and endeavors that work for concord among faiths, witness to places where they converge, or common action. On the basis of their achievements all of us are enabled to proceed. They have risked much in efforts to promote civility and peace. It is they who have witnessed to the difficulties in such ventures, have lived with frustration over what they have not achieved, and in the main been realistic about what they cannot achieve. Such pioneers

149

are often rendered suspect by traditionalist critics who fear or claim that through their taking risks or making proposals they are necessarily "giving away the store" and undercutting the integrity of particular faiths.

Most critics and some advocates of conversation among people of faith and among the religions show that they are under the impression that such conversation has been designed to find consensus, agreement on all basics. Such agreement may well be an integral part of some of the communities. Roman Catholicism and Islam, for example, picture fulfillment if and when all of the world comes to unite with them. But we are talking about the goal of those whose work transcends the boundaries of individual faith communities, even if two of them number one billion adherents. The world in which they operate is manifestly pluralist, and will remain so.

Four Philosophical Responses to Pluralism

Not only religious thinkers and agents have difficulty with pluralism and interaction when faiths collide. Philosophers do the same. While the address to the issues in theology and philosophy differ, believers can gain some wisdom from philosophers who take up the basic questions. Thus, in one of the most convincing discussions, Nicholas Rescher in a philosophical work on pluralism depicts four main sets of reactions to it, the last of them being the drive toward consensus.[1]

Rescher offers four philosophical responses. The first of these, to which we have paid too little attention, is skepticism. Skeptics, of course, rule out all religious alternatives. Second is syncretism, which contends that all the alternatives should be accepted; "all those seemingly discordant positions are in fact justified; they must, somehow, be conjoined and juxtaposed." Rescher pictures syncretism as deliberately sought; it can come accidentally. Some fusion or mixing of elements is inevitable in a pluralist society, even when participants may be hostile to each other.

150

So vivid are the wrestlings with syncretism in our time that a historian and philosopher of culture, Peter Burke, in his *Varieties of Cultural History*, has found good reason to play with synonyms and analogues. I introduce them here to show how many cultures interact to produce the new lexicon and the variety of options:

> A great variety of terms are used in different places and different disciplines to describe the processes of cultural borrowing, appropriation, exchange, reception, transfer, negotiation, resistance, syncretism, acculturation, enculturation, inculturation, transculturation, hybridization (*mestizaje*), creolization, and the interaction and interpenetration of cultures. [Also "mudejarism."][2]

Some of these terms may sound exotic, and even barbarous. Their variety bears eloquent witness to the fragmentation of today's academic world. They also reveal, Burke says, "a new conception of culture as bricolage, in which the processes of appropriation and assimilation are not marginal but central."

Rescher's third philosophical alternative he calls indifferent relativism, in which only one alternative is and should be accepted, but where acceptance arises only from "a matter of taste, of 'personal inclination,' or social tradition, or some such."

All three of these reactions are widely held among many religious people. The fourth, his choice, comes close to outlining what observers note when representatives of faiths in collision choose to come together. In this claim, "Only one alternative should be accepted," but the basis for acceptance "may differ perspectivally, from group to group, era to era, and school to school." In the theological case, while reason will play its part, rational adjudication is not the only instrument at work. As with philosophical issues, the perspective and coloration of the engagement comes from contexts, as in the case of communities and traditions. Keeping such perspectives in mind is one way to guard against skepticism, syncretism, and indifferent relativism.

Rescher's philosophical conclusion appears in a highly concentrated paragraph which is best quoted in full, since it describes a situation which offers parallels to religion:

An individual need not be intimidated by the fact of disagreement –
it makes perfectly good sense for people to do their rational best
toward securing evidentiated beliefs and justifiable choices without
undue worry about whether or not others disagree. And it is fallaci-
ous to insist on a quest for consensus on the grounds that dissensus
and pluralism are rationally intolerable. A community that exhibits
and accepts internal disagreements is in principle perfectly viable – it
makes perfectly good sense for a society to refrain from seeking to
constrain agreement in matters of opinion, valuation, and choice,
and to let a productive rivalry of discord prevail within communally
manageable and excess-avoiding limits.

 . . . For groups, a sensibly restrained situation of dissensual pluralism
should prove not only acceptable but even (within limits) advantageous – not only because the stimulus or rivalry can provide the goad
to progress, but also because a benevolent acquiescence in differences
helps the community to flourish, and because an other-respective
spirit of live-and-let-live is inherently benign and productive.[3]

The Occasion for Theological Reflection

Whether they are resistant or syncretistic, when people who make
up religious communities come into conflict, or when strangers meet
strangers, they do not only act. Like Rescher's philosophers, they
think. They may act to kill, exile, converse with, or embrace those
who are religiously different. But since faith has to do with more
than action and emotion, they regularly have to reflect on what their
ways of dealing with "the other" have to do with intellectual and
spiritual commitments that they hold, or held, before their encounter.
What they think will have much to do with how they act: if they
cannot find ways to square their actions with their deepest beliefs
and commitments, the whole situation will become unstable. The
word that theistic religions have used for their reflection, their
making of frameworks, drawing up proposals, or coming to conclusions, is theology.

This paragraph of apology has to be brief. I know and I want partners in conversation and interaction among the faiths to recognize that I know this: theology is not a congenial term to the numerous religions (Mahayana Buddhism, Unitarian Universalism, and the like) which do not witness to God or insist on such witness. Similarly, it is not a natural term from Islamic or Jewish reflectors on religious meanings. Some protest that it is imposed upon them and is a barrier to communication, its use a sign of insensitivity. But efforts to replace it force one to use ungainly constructs such as "reflection on religious experience, meanings, and texts." Here it refers to such reflection, though it is at home where faiths speak of *theos*, of God.

So, only with apologies, will we speak henceforth of theology and begin by proposing a definition for the present context. Theology in the sense that we are using the word is reflection on the life of a people in the light of a transcendent reference, which usually means whatever is grasped as the subject of revelation or enlightenment within the community. It differs from philosophy of religion because it must always involve people, while philosophy, often abstracted from experience, needs only one person, the thinker.

Theological Alternatives

Raimundo Pannikar, who has devoted his professional life to the study of how religions interact, has thought through and pointed to some logical theological options. They roughly parallel what Rescher discerns in philosophy:

1 Only one religion is true. All the others are, at best, approximations.
2 Religions refer ultimately to the same truth although in different manners and approximations. Ultimately they are all equal.
3 All religions are false because of the falsity of their claim. There is no such ultimate destiny.

4 Each religion is true because it is the best for its adherents. Truth is subjective. *"Religion ist Privatsache."*
5 Religions are the product of history and thus both similar and different according to the historical factors that have shaped them.
6 Each religion has unique features and presents mutually incommensurable insights. Each statement of a basic experience is to be evaluated on its proper terrain and merits, because the very nature of truth is pluralistic.[4]

Most intensely religious people focus on the truth claims of their one faith and are devoted to the first option, perhaps not even thinking of others as "at best, approximations." Religious indifferentists and those who conceive of themselves as being most generous and open to positive dealings with others function on the basis of the second option, that "ultimately they are all equal."

Those devoted to the third option, the abolition of religion, may think that they have resolved the issue for their society or the globe. In the eyes of all others, this set of strangers will appear ironically and inescapably to function much as the religions, I am tempted to say "the other religions," do.

The fourth option in which "truth is subjectivity" appeals to those who see religion only in existentialist terms, but who are least ready to make their case in a pluralist society composed of groups of people who are faith-full in a variety of ways. The fifth option is in its own way environmentally deterministic to such an extent that it discourages theological reflection and commitment.

It is not necessary in a pluralist society for all to agree that these are the main options or that they are stated as fully accurate summaries. It is the character of pluralism not to demand consensus on ultimate truth claims. In private religious life, making a choice is urgent. For public purposes, those who would wish to venture forth with rationales for religious interaction, debate among the five is valuable, but not finally determinative for faith or society.

The sixth alternative, Panikkar's choice, parallels Rescher's fourth, the perspectival one, as it realistically accents "insights." That each

154

faith community has "unique features" is the most obvious fact about all of them. Now, the idea of appraising each religion "on its proper terrain and merits" will strike many as being also too environmentally and historically determinative to be entirely satisfying. But there are clues for interaction in this alternative.

Metaphysicians may debate, preachers may thunder, leaders may jostle for position, but, there being no arbiter on the scene and no means of providing access to the source of truth among the claims of religions, citizens have to combine their own commitment to "their truth," which they may see as "the truth" and find ways to live creatively with those who offer insights "incommensurable" to their own. On such a basis, they seek civil peace, the kind of peace one needs for public life, even if it is not finally metaphysically satisfying.

Incommensurable Stories

The religions do not have to be incommensurable in all their features. They may share certain themes in common. While interacting, they may find ever more of these, and such findings may inspire them to reach deeper into the reservoir of convictions that nourish their communions. But those who adhere to each as being decisive for faith and action will see their particularities in new ways. That feature was classically designated by American philosopher George Santayana who, in his book *Reason in Religion*, wrote what serves as the background to the thesis of this chapter:

> Any attempt to speak without speaking any particular language is not more hopeless than the attempt to have a religion that shall be no religion in particular . . . Thus every living and healthy religion has a marked idiosyncrasy. Its power consists in its special and surprising message and in the bias which that revelation gives to life. The vistas it opens and the mysteries it propounds are another world to live in; and another world to live in – whether we expect ever to pass wholly over into it or no – is what we mean by having a religion.[5]

In the end, when faith communities collide, both the problems and the possibilities in them come down to stories. Practices, rituals, doctrines, traditions, habits, and commands all play their part. But what prevents religions from blithely merging, what leads people to resist being blended into an undifferentiated whole, is their attachment to story. Through interpreting their stories, they "do" theology.

A trend in recent years toward writing "narrative theology," with its stress on reflection and story, has opened the door for a larger apprehension of what theology can be and who theologians are. Believing publics have often come to be suspicious of or resentful about the professionals. They often simply ignore them as ivory tower-dwellers in their remoteness or they disdain them for messing up the stories behind the faith. Literary artists, novelists, poets, and essayists have begun to supply theology as we speak of it here. So have lay people, including the humblest among them.

Questions that Arise in Theology

In our particular case, much of the theological pondering and pro-duction, informal as it may be, therefore issues from those who do not think of themselves as theologians. Basic questions inspire their reflection and their tentative answers. We will register some of them, only a few of which will be addressed here.

Thus: Does commitment to one faith community and its divine object necessarily mean the exclusion of all others from positive con-sideration? Can others outside the community formed by that story be "saved?" What do members of such a community mean when they speak of God and of persons or that community being saved? Why are some believers militant and others mild? Is it legitimate to try to convert others, to engage in proselytism?

Questions like these imply answers peculiar to each community: What can we know of the mind of God in respect to any choice to try to convert others – or to leave them alone? Is there one truth at the base of all enduring faiths? Or do they agree at rock bottom and

156

differ only in the workings-out of faith? Can the person committed to a faith that comes across as exclusive find truths in other faiths? On what terms do I practice welcoming the stranger in faith, the one who can be a menace? What elements of two or more faiths can be blended or at least rendered disarmed and congenial to the other?

Still more: How to keep a particular believing community together without defining and reflecting on its differences from others, and perhaps on its impulse to persecute or militantly engage the others? Where do concerns for afterlife come in: who gets "saved" for it and in it, and who remains in hell, purgatory, or Sheol because of personal disbelief and misbehavior? What demands are made, what commands issued, what expectations uttered, in respect to acts of justice or mercy? Listeners to the conversations of serious people in cultures shaped or tinged by almost any particular religion will hear such questions.

To the point: If my community is open to welcoming the stranger, how shall we conceive of and justify the choices that are made? This is the focal question about religions in pluralistic societies. Believers pose them in today's North America, the British Isles, Western and increasingly Eastern Orthodox Europe, especially secularized places such as France, Germany, the Netherlands, or extensions of European culture in places like Australia or wherever Western missions have effectively operated, and in selected areas in Africa and Asia. Christian theology lives on in the semi-secular West even where Christendom, an institution and culture of power, gets progressively passed by. And, living on, it influences believers and non-believers alike.

The point of stringing together this set of apparently randomly formed and placed questions is to lead to this: all the religions respond to such questions by referring to old stories or telling new ones. They may engage in philosophical reflection and discourse about these, connect them to a metaphysic, and systematize them into dogmas. But story stands behind each, and these stories in the end point to incommensurable visions of reality.

157

American theologian John B. Cobb, Jr., has been a pioneer among those who seek both to keep the integrity of the faiths, of his faith, and profoundly to engage the other. As he canvasses the range of options, he first summarizes the approach of the most notable twentieth-century Roman Catholic theologian, Karl Rahner, who taught that God works salvifically everywhere. Cobb writes that for Rahner, "People can be saved whether or not they are related to the Catholic Church or consciously accept Jesus Christ. People saved in this way he calls anonymous Christians. The religions of the world are used by God in this salvific work," but are not on a par with the Christian church. Other Catholics who are open to encounter, Cobb notes, find this approach too arrogant. Thus Hans Küng, another prominent Catholic, has written: "God saves Hindus as Hindus, not as anonymous Christians." The mission of the church in his eyes is to be of service to other religions. While official Catholicism is far from this position, Cobb notes that Pope Paul VI and the Vatican Secretariat in its engagement with Islam often lean toward such a view. The Secretariat draws short of saying the church has to learn from others, since it has the full truth. Yet it advocates open conversation to promote understanding. In the face of these, Cobb states his own "creed":

> My central thesis here is that for Christianity to be, and to remain to the end, one among others does not involve its relativization in the destructive sense in which this is now felt by so many. It does relativize every form taken by Christianity in time. It does not relativize the process of creative transformation by which it lives and which it knows as Christ.
>
> At another level and in another sense, however, that too must be recognized as one principle by which one community lives alongside other principles by which other communities live. This is a funda- mental theological problem for the Christian. As a Christian I believe that Christ is the way, the truth, and the life and that no one comes to know God except through Christ. Does that mean after all that I am rejecting pluralism? I do not think so.[6]

158

What Cobb does think he details by relating "the way, the truth, and the life" in Christ as being "bound up with creative transformation." Tantalizing as that proposal and definition are, following through on them is not integral to the present argument. It is illustrative of the point that there are ways to keep the integrity of one's own community and commitment and relate to others in disarming and positive ways. It is the negative side of the proposal that concerns us most in a treatise on the menace of strangers' faiths.

The Question of Lethal Theologies

In that context, the first natural question for many believers in most ages, shocking to some but surprisingly frequent today, is: Does God want me to kill or not to kill, to denigrate or not to denigrate, the strangers and their communities in other faiths? To those in a republic for whom faith is a domestic and domesticated, tamed and tame matter, where tolerance, relativism, and indifference prevail among majorities, it seems bizarre even to raise such questions. Yet whoever looks out at the wars, conflicts, guerrilla actions, and murderous individual interactions that make headlines today will find that millions are poised to kill those who are strangers to them, and many do. One need only invoke the ghosts, shades, and murderous potential of al-Qaeda, the partisans in Northern Ireland or in the former Yugoslavia, and of many inter-tribal wars such as among the Tutsi and Hutus in Africa, to see how common such killing is today. The history of religions often appears to be little more than the history of conflict among those who are strange to each other.

So strong has this emphasis been and so strong is it in areas of unrest and revolution today that cynical and suspicious critics who gaze on those religions that profess tolerance and support pluralistic society often taunt them by saying something like "Real religion has to be persecutory. If you really believed, as the militants do who show readiness to be killed for their faith, you would kill, too."

159

Such taunting is not new. The classic statement by a liberal who cannot conceive of religious groups living in positive ways with each other and then contributing together to the common good was written by Walter Lippmann, who in 1929 wrote about relativism within pluralism in *A Preface to Morals*:

> The existence of rival sects, the visible demonstration that none has a monopoly, the habit of neutrality, cannot but dispose men against an unquestioning acceptance of the authority of one sect. So many faiths, so many loyalties, are offered to the modern man that at last none seems to him wholly inevitable and fixed in the order of the universe. The existence of many churches in one community weakens the foundation of all of them. And that is why every church in the heyday of its power proclaims itself to be catholic and intolerant.[7]

Lippmann's belief that pluralism must weaken religious commitment is belied by the fact that the increase of pluralism has not led to a decline in faith, at least not in many societies. Relatively homogeneous nations in Western Europe, be they Catholic or Lutheran or Reformed in their modern origins, have seen more decline in religious measurements than have America and other places which are host to diverse groups, and long have been such.

While the perceptions behind arguments such as those of Lippmann characteristically issue from historically formed or informed humanists, they obviously have a theological basis. The questioner and the taunter alike are asking: What is the character of the One you call God? In the texts which are your resources, animators, and monitors, what does this God say and do? How are you called to obedience to this God? Through what means, for example, which scriptures, are you notified sufficiently about the divine will that you might attack others in this God's name, or that you might refrain from doing so?

Without question, those in the biblical tradition who promote tolerance have some squirming to do when they read a Lippmann. There are some texts which relate the hidden God Israel worshiped to a presence in other communities – as the writing of the prophet

Amos did. But more of them depict God as jealous, particular, revealed as someone who warns against and punishes those who turn to other gods, or who import images of such gods into Israel. The errant idolaters may prosper for a while, but eventually God or God's avengers will attack and destroy. The revelation of the jealous God who is also the agent of shalom who desires reconciliation among strangers, appears as a minority if ultimately convincing note.

Wishing those texts away will not lead to their excision. They remain, to challenge and haunt latter-day believers. Participants in biblical traditions who wish to enter the field of pluralistic discourse have to draw on the pictures of God who says: "Vengeance is mine, I will repay." Such texts warn against licensing people through all times and places to arrogate to themselves the personality and pre-rogatives of this jealous God. Those who respond to the Bible find it urgent to reflect on these narratives. What might have been explicable, if not justifiable, when Israel was taking shape, dare hardly be the main note about God in a time where surveillance and weaponry are efficient instruments for murderous religions. Many biblical stories, including those about endorsed figures such as Abraham and David, tell of people who would be anything but heroes today for their murderous deeds against strangers in the name of God.

Taking Religion Out of the Public Realm

Another framework that provokes theology relates to the decision to ignore differences or work to keep religion out of the public sphere, letting it go unnoticed. "Religion is a private affair," in that case, becomes a widely heard slogan. Since faith is a private matter, what the stranger believes is no concern of mine. The stranger and I will try to keep a distance from each other, bottling up our own textual interpretations, and letting all go their own ways.

That division of life into spheres worked better when religion was more credibly viewed as a private affair. Today, while it certainly has not lost its personal and private appeal, religion is highly public.

It is evident in the prosecution of war and peace, in violence and reconciliation. One confronts its images in the arts and entertainment world. In any case, it certainly is no stranger to politicians in a world where "faith-based" enterprises are not confined to the United States.

The choice systematically to ignore religion is a decision that often has a theological dimension. It is rooted in a determination that strangers pose no menace and provide no opportunity, so decisions about them are irrelevant. Those who choose to ignore differences are giving embodiment to the notion that God does not care and would not care for souls and ways of life. Live and let live may be a feature of a way of life into which one casually drifts. But when decisions about this feature become subjects of reflection, vision narrows and moral energy gets sapped.

Those who care about moral, intellectual, and spiritual choices may not wish to intrude systematically on the lives and ways of the stranger. But to decide to ignore these choices and thus the people who make them may give the impression that one does not take one's own way seriously and does not care about the neighbor at all. Most of us who enjoy life in free republics have little immediate experience of aggressive acts by proselytizers or persecutors and may find it fanciful even to bring up the subject. Yet significant minorities close to home are aggressive, and we live in a world where hundreds of millions act belligerently in the name of their faith – or are victims of those who do. Hence, even to reflect on serious matters while in situations of luxury and ease becomes urgent. Not to decide about religion in public life is to decide.

The Impulse to Convert, to Proselytize

Having just mentioned proselytizing, I have to follow through on another theological issue, the one that connects with it.[8] The alternative to ignoring and avoiding faith in the public world can mean attempting to convert the stranger. This can occur through overt evangelizing or through subtler, more seductive and gradualist means.

162

In such cases, members of some group or other have reflected and judged that God is on the side of their bearing witness. This can mean representing the truth at whatever cost in human relations while one aspires to diminish the company of strangers while enlarging the community of belongers.

Such efforts have characterized those Christian and Islamic communities that have been defined as exclusive and aggressive through most of their centuries of existence. Missionary faiths conceive of the gods of others as false and even evil. Portraying the God of the other only in negative terms, they try to counter the influence of the worship of such a God, and set out to present or impose their own way as being the only right and true one. That way of describing the impulse to evangelize is one-sided and even cruel. For millions of believers, to reach out to the stranger in efforts to convert them and welcome them into a host community is an act of love. They conceive of it as an attempt to rescue another person from desperate fates in this world and that to come.

In many ages such proselytization was a simpler matter in most cultures, since it was possible to portray the other faiths as simply wicked, as proven by examination of the wickedness of the adherents. The believer decided: I will not drive the stranger off or try to kill him, but to win him. Some will see all efforts that flow from such thinking to be offensive, exploitative, at least ill-mannered, and perhaps dangerous. Yet the agent of efforts to convert will proceed as if no criticism was valid. Nothing in human affairs is as important to them as winning the soul of the stranger, concern over the tactics be hanged. Still, efforts to minimize the abrasion between faith communities have made some progress. One thinks of Roman Catholicism, which still claims full truth uniquely for itself but recognizes divine activity and partial truth in others.

A corollary to the issue of proselytizing is how up-front and upsetting participants in conversation across the lines of faith may be. That word "may" sounds unnecessary and use of it futile. Those who take pride in being offensive will not be reined in or policed by outside forces. The concern here is to promote thought and rethinking by those who bring articulate positions to their encounters. They differ vastly from each other.

Some Jewish communities have forbidden conversation and activity by Jews with other faiths, in efforts to protect the integrity of their faith by remaining in isolation. It is also hard to conceive of a Muslim who would muffle Islamic witness for the sake of understanding among the faiths. Many Christians express what one well calls macho attitudes against other Christians who are not aggressive in efforts to convert others. Christians who encourage conversation among faiths are of several minds. Some argue that the cause is best furthered if all are cautious about stories that others may regard as offensive.

To keep the record straight in a manifesto, I am close to the company of thinkers such as the Anglicans John V. Taylor and Lesslie Newbigin, the Baptist E. Luther Copeland, and many Catholic veteran missiologists who stress that Christians in conversation with others need not set aside basic Christian commitments and do their partners in such discourse no favor by doing so. They only create confusion and postpone the time when differences have to be and get to be articulated. We can access Taylor and Newbigin through summaries by Copeland.

Taylor "insists that what God did in Jesus Christ, particularly in the cross, was necessary for the salvation of all persons everywhere." And, here is the complex point: "he believes that 'this kind of statement is appropriate for dialogue, whether coming from Christians or adherents of other religions.'" He says that all religions have their "jealousies," and points out that all, Hindus, Buddhists, Muslims, Jews, or Christians, "must by necessity believe that their own faith has universal finality."

Lesslie Newbigin goes even further, asking Christians to tell the story of Jesus in their conversations among the faiths. Copeland prefers the concept of "confessing," a less threatening word than "witness" in such conversations.

Copeland confesses that through years of encounters across the lines of faith communities, which means with Jains, Sikhs, and Jews as strangers, he acquired a better understanding of such religions than before and came to appreciate his own at a deeper level. The concept of evangelizing by strangers will itself be one of those "jealousies" that have to be set on the table – in front of people from other faiths who do something similar.

To change the rules of the game and have representatives of one faith seek to convert the others, when all parties have covenanted for conversation, however, ruins all possibility of true exchange and learning. Efforts to convert would have to follow their own rules, and not be disruptive of other kinds of discourse around the table. Such efforts are in any case likely to be counterproductive, since such tactics would suggest what Gabriel Marcel described as implying a loathsome image of God. Such a God would be seen as having followers prey and pounce on others when they are off-guard. Ruling out all contexts for evangelizing, however, would keep from the table many potential participants who can advance the purposes of interaction.[9]

Theological Universalisms and Particularisms

We return to another alternative envisioned in philosophy by Rescher and in theology by Panikkar, since it has become central to the agenda of those, particularly Christians, who engage in theological reflection on pluralism. While this book is mainly about civil pluralism, theological pluralism hovers in the background and presses itself forward as an issue. This concludes in a theological move to pronounce all religions as one at base. That means following through with strategies to see this commitment realized in structures, organizations, and ways of life. The belonger and the stranger, it is declared in advance, are one, but they do not know it. They suffer from an overlay of competitive institutions and demands, and they follow petty policies encrusted by historical experience but lacking warrants today. Strip away these overlays and encrustations, it is said, and you will find revealed the warm and pulsing heart of all-religions-as-essentially-one. All a community need do, in the counsel that issues from this theology, is to move from sectarian particularism to an embrace of the uniting and single whole faith as fancied.

For universalists, people who generously want to abolish all lines that keep strangers in estrangement, such a declaration that all religions are one or should aspire to become one has much allure. They often express disappointment or scorn for those who do not share this vision or pursue its strategies. For them, theological conversation has the single goal of finding ways to overcome all meaningful differences.

These universalists meet opposition among particularists, who are doing their own reflecting. Particularists are the anti-utopian realists. They know that inside history the idea that all religions will freely agree on common tenets and live a common life is unrealistic. The trend of the century past toward ecumenical life within broad communions, where understandings have grown across the boundaries of faiths, has now met a strong counter-trend. As we noted, in open contests anywhere in the world, liberal, tolerant, concessive religions and faith communities that work toward the merger of all the faiths are outpaced and effectively countered by militant definers, fundamentalists, and traditionalists. That fact does not make the extremely particularist contenders right. It does point to the fact that simple universalists overlook kinds of commitments with which in more moderate forms they do well to reckon.

In the eyes of most people, religion is not something imposed from headquarters, from vaticans or bureaucracies or by governmental will. It is of the heart, and that means that those who hold it have "dug in" locally. Those who assess that it would be hard to convince Muslims at Mecca to unite with a tolerant Jewish or Christian group will tell you that on the local level the commitments to particular worldviews can be especially intense. Those who are bound to them are not candidates for being merged into an ill-defined whole that lacks their stories.

Thus, much of Islam has the character of a village religion, even when its adherents migrate to the cities. As with other faiths, this one gets passed on from parents to children through complex rites. These rites don't match those of any other faith community, and those who stage the rites do not expect they ever will. Therefore, observers of this phenomenon are likely to ask, why try?

They may also raise a second question: Who determines and defines the emergent or winning religion after any contention? Some who are responding to this question have gone to work with the hope of producing a single, united theology and community. But ironically they have in almost every case succeeded only in producing one more small and usually precious particular religion. Such will seem to most people to be harder to grasp and less alluring than the story-driven faiths that will remain competitors to the universalists.

Some efforts at fabricating the single united faith have been not merely innocuous but disastrous. The best-known instance in recent times is a kind of synthetic faith propounded by world historian Arnold Toynbee, who in the middle of the last century enjoyed a vogue. In choosing which elements should be a part of the emerging world religious synthesis that he was promoting, Toynbee dismissed Judaism as an antique and even fossilized religion that had nothing to say to the emerging interactive world. His star subsequently sank as rapidly as if he had used Judaism as his base and dismissed other faiths as fossilized.

The bottom line or first word from theological critics of the idea of one religion is: it cannot happen. It wouldn't work. The price is too high and the product too emotionally unsatisfying. Such a vision lies beyond history, as for Christians some New Testament letters and the Apocalypse testify and project.

Theology Impelling Conversation

The next strategy that demands theological rationalization has something in common with the one just mentioned: that is, to enter a conversation in which effort is made to find some common elements of the religions and to dismiss what are presumed to be irrelevancies

167

in the pursuit of public and common goods. In a way this was the civil proposal of the American founder Benjamin Franklin, who admired what he believed all the faiths held in common, something that when he was finished defining it curiously matched his own Deist creed. He dismissed the particulars. It is true that such forms labeled "civil religion," "public religion," or "religion of a republic" do coexist, often creatively, with particular faiths. But to critics, these forms are quickly perceived as one more such particular faith, and a seductive competitor that must be opposed. Franklin's creed was in the end as metaphysically based as was that of the Presbyterians whom he opposed.

The intentions to form a religious synthesis out of the common elements in all the faiths are not always directed to policies for civil societies. Advocates often describe them also as aesthetically pleasing because their abrasive edges are gone. They would presumably be advertised as ethically satisfying because publics that employed them could therefore agree on the basis from which they would argue for specific ethical outcomes. They are envisioned and advertised as being attractive to the soul by those who will seek "wholeness" and do not want to be distracted by concern over trivia. This proposal had the double appeal that came with invention: it had newness in its favor. And it was designed to appeal psychologically to people who cherish elements of their own tradition while they are dissatisfied with most other parts of it.

When faiths avoid collision and come to mutual understanding, this does not ordinarily occur so that they can present a common phalanx against the non-religious. The religious talk to other religious, the strangers, especially for one positive and one negative reason. Positively, the insights of each can enrich the other, and adherents will benefit. In my own career this kind of thing has been most visible in respect to the understandings of health, medicine, suffering, and the passages of life. Judaism and Christianity were born as healing cults. Their prophets, psalmists, parable tellers, and in the Christian case, their messiah, were healers and teachers of healing. When modern technological medicine developed, many believers began to neglect their origins and development. Then, late in the twentieth century, many adventurers in the West began to experiment with what came to be called alternative medicine. Such medicine has many sources, sometimes including in the brains of charlatans and quacks. Others grew out of "new religions," which usually picked up motifs from the older ones. But most of the important and enduring experiments came from encounters between Jews and Christians and Hinduism, Buddhism, and other living embodiments of ancient faiths. For some in the West this engagement resulted in a spiritual awakening that was born of distaste for what they had known in their own faith community. Some manifested envy for what they perceived others possessed, and made efforts to make up for lost time by converting to the other faiths. The Bantu people in Africa have a saying: "He who never visits thinks his mother is the only cook."[10] Now they "traveled" and learned new spiritual cuisines. Later, one can report, many returned to that figurative mother's kitchen, their consciousness having been altered but not so much that they could not still find a home there. Now they could spread a more elaborate table in their efforts at healing.

So much for the positive example. The other reason has a more negative but still creative character. Think of it as damage control. Carrying on common conversational and activist pursuits among the faiths can promote enough understanding and common vision to minimize the damage faiths might do to other faiths and to the world around them if they remain in isolation and ignorance.

In the 1970s, while serving as an associate dean in a graduate divinity school at a university, I found that my job description included raising funds to support research by faculty and students in the advanced study of religion. As I set out on one of my missions I asked a congenial colleague to give me something to serve as a rationale. In a world of misery and urgent physical needs, on what grounds should I appeal for such funds? He answered: "For the same reason we went out years before to get funding for advanced studies of sexuality. Religion is a lot like sex: if you get it wrong, there is real trouble."

Few participants in endeavors to converse and work across the lines of faith communities are so naive as to picture utopia beckoning as a result of their efforts. Sometimes, as stranger meets stranger, increased familiarity instead produces increased contempt. One party discerns secrets, weaknesses, and often malign features in the faith of the other, and consequently feels a need to turn defensive. Or one may stand just sufficiently outside the understanding of the other's faith to fail to be able to do justice to it. But not to make the effort can be worse.

In the current conflict among Muslims and Christians, it is true that extremist elements unrepresentative of each are firebrands and some, particularly among the former, have become international terrorists. They will not enter conversations and have no impulse to understand those who are strangers to them. They have chosen what Lifton called the "constrictive" approach to faith and life, and pursue it radically. They have done so partly in their fear of having to deal with the protean temptations that come with spiritual openness.

If the hardliners will not come to the table of conversation, the slightly more moderate traditionalists may do so. In fact, interactions have often yielded most when they begin in least obviously promising settings. Those described as liberals, modernists, or people with a reputation for tolerance have their place at the table: without them there would never have been these efforts. But the more conservative representatives also introduce notes of realism with which the various parties have to reckon. And when such apparently intransigent sorts from both or all camps meet, they may make some contribution to an understanding out of which a safer and more peaceful world can emerge.

As most wars in the new millennium relate to religious sources or overlays, anything that has the possibility of improving understanding merits support. When the West misreads the meaning of jihad or the Muslim world identifies rhetoric from the West with the medieval idea of crusade, a dangerous miscommunication is going on.

I would not want to oversell the case for dramatic outcomes. Those who have gone out raising funds for graduate study of religion can help those who want to understand the dangerous side of religion in order to help minimize the damage they would otherwise do. But few of them would be so naive or arrogant as to propose that they have solutions to the problems that too readily issue in war and terrorism. However, they can deal with the masses of ordinary believers where they cannot reach the firebrands or convert the fanatics, and thus can make some contributions in the realm of spirit and mind.

On Theological Pluralism

Relations among communities appear within a framework of four main policies: exclusivism, pluralism, inclusivism, and, more recently, mutual acceptance.[11] Exclusivism is easiest to document and hardest to penetrate. Those who hold to it regard themselves as the proper belongers, even if they have been temporarily displaced by strangers who must be removed. Many of the revolutions on Islamic soil are of this sort: "we" were given this place by the revelation of Allah and Allah gave us rules for being stewards of the place and all of its people. Now, as in the case of Algeria, but also of Egypt at the end of Gamal Abdel Nasser's rule, radical Islamists have appeared on the scene. They regard the rulers in such regimes as heretical, apostate, or, worst of all, compromising. The Muslim Brotherhood, formed in 1928, began an explicit attempt to retake the land from Muslim strangers.

Theological pluralists, secondly, in most summations, are seen as more or less hospitably ready to be open to greeting the stranger. They find that they and the stranger believe in relatively the same things, or that they have enough common ground to show that all the serious faiths merit hearing because they represent different ways of making similar contributions to civil or global society. A severe critic of these synthesizers, Anglican theologian Gavin D'Costa, observed that the Enlightenment, "in granting a type of equality to all religions, ended up denying public truth to any and all of them."

This critic concludes, naming John Hick, Paul Knitter, and Dan Cohn-Sherbok: "Their god is modernity's god."[12]

Among the critics of pluralism, the Enlightenment is regularly the bogey. It represents to them a philosophy that, while tending to reduce all religions to a similar level, ends up in effect in becoming a new kind of religion itself. Historian Crane Brinton observed that in the late seventeenth century there arose "what seems to clearly be a new religion," which he called "simply Enlightenment, with a capital E."[13] Less ready to call it a religion but seeing the problems it posed for the religions was Alasdair MacIntyre, who defined the "Enlightenment project" so decisively that, once made aware of his strictures, defenders of pluralism had to reckon with it and come up with some sort of reply. John Horton and Susan Mendus summarize his major work, *After Virtue*:

> The Enlightenment project which has dominated philosophy during the past three hundred years promised a conception of rationality independent of historical and social context, and independent of any specific understanding of man's nature or purpose. But not only has that promise in fact been unfulfilled, the project is itself fundamentally flawed and the promise could never be fulfilled. In consequence, modern moral and political thought are in a state of disarray from which they can be rescued only if we revert to an Aristotelian paradigm, with its essential commitment to teleology, and construct an account of practical reason premised on that commitment.[14]

It would be tempting to pause at this point and argue with the second half of the MacIntyre critique of the Enlightenment project, particularly to question his own exclusivist turn to Aristotle, but the first half of what he wrote is much to the point for present purposes.

Gavin D'Costa summarizes the theologically pluralist option in ways that are congenial to our understanding and purposes:

> By "pluralist" I mean a range of features, shared by writers who use this term of self-description, to indicate the broad assumption that: all religions (with qualifications) lead to the same divine reality; there

is no privileged self-manifestation of the divine; and finally, religious harmony will follow if tradition-specific (exclusivist) approaches which allegedly claim monopoly over the truth are abandoned in favor of pluralist approaches which recognize that all religions display the truth in differing ways.[15]

Inclusivists, in turn, argue they should be the rightful belongers, and that others may be welcome because, when they probe, they will find points of congruence at their depth with these inclusivists. Unlike the pluralists, they do not agree with the "more or less" equal principle among the faiths. They are like the exclusivists in many ways, claiming as they do a complete hold on the complete truth. But unlike exclusivists and with the pluralists, they are generous in making clear their belief that strangers who take other paths, which means follow other faiths, may also well be "right." D'Costa ingeniously argues that exclusivists and inclusivists arrive at similar places.

That leaves the "acceptance" model. It introduces a note which exclusivists and many pluralists may find threatening, since it carries the case for hospitality so far that all claims for superiority by participants when faith communities encounter each other are to be willingly suppressed. As Paul Knitter presents it, models for a theology of religions, in the main,

> either so stress the particularity of one religion that the validity of all others is jeopardized . . . or they stress the universal validity of [all religions] all in a way that fogs over the real particular differences . . . The Acceptance Model thinks it can do a better job at this balancing act . . . It does so not by holding up the superiority of any one religion, nor by searching for that common something that makes them all valid, but by accepting the real diversity of all faiths. The religious traditions of the world are really different, and we have to accept those differences.[16]

That such a model causes difficulty for many in "particular" religions, such as Catholic or evangelical, is obvious, and following the "acceptance" proposal carries us beyond the scope of this manifesto.

The Vatican has disciplined some theologians in these ranks, and non-Catholic Christians, who would have their counterparts in other religions, also have difficulty with both the intention and the outcome of this "balancing act." Yet it is an option of which people in Knitter's version of the "postmodern" world have to be aware and which the theologians among them will find themselves considering.

The case of Christian evangelicalism is of special importance and best illuminates the stresses that occur when members of an enclave faith of belongers choose to interact with the faiths of strangers. Timothy C. Tennent surprised those who were less familiar with changes in evangelicalism with his full-ranged discussion of evangelical conversations with Hinduism, Buddhism, and Islam.[17] Often overlooked because of the head start that Catholics and mainstream Protestants had held, evangelicals, thanks to their missionary presence and aspirations, had much at stake as they began to appraise ways of living with those to whom they were the foreigners in the worlds of Hindus, Buddhists, and Muslims.

Edinburgh professor Tennent, who teaches also in America and India, keeps his eye on four worlds. He must first deal with the evangelical majority that disdains engagement with the stranger in religion, perhaps at the expense of their earlier feelings of superiority. He quotes Grace Buford, a scholar of Buddhism, who believes that some Christian participants do lean too far. A chapter title in one of her books is "If the Buddha Is So Great, Why Are These People Christians?" Tennent was not ready to go so far that she had to ask him such a question. At one point he even argued that leaders in other religions become frustrated when Christians give away too much and capitulate too generously to others. With their reservations and strictures in mind, he had to provide a rationale for every step he took. Tennent criticized fellow evangelicals and other conservative Christians for their "safety box" approach, which, he charged, they had designed to preserve the gospel. Therefore, they lock it up and do not encounter others.

Tennent would not retain credentials as an evangelical if he did not take some swings at liberal participants for failing to defend

Christianity. He counters them by saying that unless the partner in conversation has a faith commitment, people of other faiths will not be attracted. They will simply be confused. Nor would he be in evangelical style did he not criticize liberals for relativism, or for the assertion with which he charges them, not accurately in most cases, that all religions are basically the same. Liberals as Christians get scored for renouncing all efforts to convert people of other faiths. Tennent is aware that those who in openness approach truths in other faiths are making their presence known in evangelical Christianity, often by borrowing ideas from Catholics. While he identifies himself as one who will yield on no distinctives, he calls himself an engaged exclusivist. As such he would emulate Martin Luther in his Table Talk, whom Tennent saw as believing that "give and take" in "informal non-combatant" ways edifies all who participate.

Most of the energy put into the pluralist conversation has come from Catholic, Protestant, Evangelical, and Enlightenment sources. In the West, the absence of Judaism from this roster is at first startling, given Jews' ready and sometimes urgent willingness to participate in conversation and activity. D'Costa could find only one work by a Jewish pluralist, Dan Cohn-Sherbok.[18] Some Jews are pluralist in respect to various forms of Christianity, to which they discern many foundational ties, but this is less the case in respect to Hinduism and the like.

Cohn-Sherbok's criticism of exclusivism and inclusivism is predictable; it is his commitment to pluralism that enriches our analysis. Like Christian and other pluralists, he deals with the historical phenomenon: the "sweep of Jewish history thus points to a new goal – a global vision of the universe of faiths in which Judaism is perceived as one among many paths to the Divine." The evidence he adduces is selective, and most Jewish scholars would have a different reading of this "sweep," though they may agree in some of his choices of instances.

Cohn-Sherbok brings up two features in Jewish theology. The first he supports to promote ethics: "In contemporary society the Jewish

175

community needs to adopt an even more open stance towards the world religions." Secondly, Jews accepting pluralism find that it "paves the way for encounter on the deepest levels." In the end his proposal bears little of a distinctive Jewish character. Along with Catholic and Protestant pluralism, his approach blends well into the Enlightenment version. He also finally sidesteps the issue of truth: "In the end the Jewish Pluralist must remain agnostic about the correctness of his own religious convictions." Fair-mindedly, he equally relativizes other faiths: "Neither Jew, Muslim, Christian, Hindu, nor Buddhist has any justification for believing that his respective tradition embodies the uniquely true and superior religious path."

Less fair-mindedly, Cohn-Sherbok broke the rules of his own game and made "intolerant" judgments of his own and other faiths, using some norm or other – his critics, like D'Costa, say the Enlightenment or modernity's theology. Nor has he tried to understand why people who profess these faiths take pains to do so. They do not have to believe in "unique truth" or "superior religion," but they would have to believe that the faith they profess has qualities that distinctively work for their salvation and interpretation of life.

Where Does the Risk of Hospitality Lead?

Theologies of pluralism are most satisfying to liberal thinkers in the various faiths, while popular versions of these color the interpretation of great numbers of moderate folks in each. There is great resistance to these as instruments through which bridging among faiths can occur if they are to ensure the integrity of the separate traditions and the stories by which they live. Realists can applaud the intellectual endeavors of theologians of pluralism, but they are also ready to recognize that for foreseeable and probably long-term futures, the faith communities, for all their erosion, the buffeting they take in postmodernity, the indifference that gnaws at them, and the subtle syncretisms through which they adapt to the world around them, are too satisfying, too rewarding to the millions who

176

make them up, for any of them to be ready to be written off like Toynbee's "fossilized" Jews, or merged by synthesizers.

If the realist vision prevails, some might ask why put so much energy into risking hospitality, welcoming the stranger, and starting the conversation. The realist also knows how difficult and important that start is. Whoever deals with profound divisions, warring religious groups, and estranged parties who have become entrenched, has to treat the opening of the door as almost miraculous.

As for the need for miracles at beginnings, a cherished story is a reminder. Paul Elmen tells it:

> When Cardinal de Polignac told Madame du Deffand that the martyr St. Denis, the first Bishop of Paris, had walked a hundred miles carrying his head in his hand, Madame du Deffand correctly observed, "In such a promenade it is the first step that is difficult."[19]

Lacking faith in miracles of such a sort need not breed a skepticism about the possibility of good things happening in the name of religious encounters. We have concentrated on engagement across the lines of religious factions and between faith communities, since restoring old ties or effecting new ones is so difficult and yet potentially so rewarding. To get French Muslims and French secularists to begin to meet and hear each other, and to probe the myths and stories of the other, is difficult enough. To get African Anglican bishops and North American Episcopal bishops, united in ecclesiastical life but bitterly divided over the issue of homosexuality, to do the same may seem more difficult. We have not even undertaken analysis of the Arab–Israeli, often Muslim–Jewish conflict in the Middle East, since it falls beyond the scope of this endeavor.

Mention of efforts to envision better ways in that final instance, however, suggests that it is not in place to give up in circumstances that look hopeless and seem to need miracles. People of good will put energies into changing such situations, often in ways congruent with themes of "belongers" and "strangers" – think of the Land issue there; the need to move beyond tolerance to the risk of hospitality;

the possibility that lies in myth and story both to divide and to unite.

Thus Marc Gopin, in a daring book that some would regard as optimistic, advances the issue of shared myth and ritual in creative ways. From exploration of the uniting and dividing myth of Abraham that underlies the developments of both peoples and the rituals consequent to such stories, Gopin listened to people and summarized: "This conflict reveals some basic ways in which mythic constructs and competing stories and rituals frame this conflict in very profound ways." He goes on to insist that "an inseparability of religion and culture in this conflict . . . presents both challenges and opportunities." The cultures are dynamic, not static. He calls for "a creative investigation and experimentation with the vast reservoir of Abrahamic uses of ritual to heal, to establish basic patterns suggesting civility, to transform broken relations, to mourn, to repent, to end war, and to make peace":

> We must bring the issues of peace and conflict into innovative spaces of human engagement, such as the street, the public space, an area that has been engaged historically by cultural and religious traditions but is utterly neglected by the abstractions of contemporary approaches to coexistence. The public space matters. The human face in the public space matters.[20]

The programs of Marc Gopin and other practical dreamers include second and third steps and more than those St. Denis took on his "most difficult" hundred mile walk. The problem with the St. Denis story is that the martyr's head had been severed and life was gone. So long as the human face is welcomed in the public space, there is life. Faiths will continue to collide, but those individuals and groups that risk hospitality and promote engagement with the stranger, the different, the other, will contribute to a world in which measured hopes can survive and those who hope can guide.

Notes

Chapter 1 Religious Strangers as Menaces

1 Annual reports issue from the World Evangelization Research Center, http://www.gem-werc.org/; these figures are the center's estimates for mid-2002.
2 William E. Connolly, *The Ethos of Pluralization* (Minneapolis: University of Minnesota Press, 1995), p. xxii.

Chapter 2 "Belongers" versus Strangers

1 See the five volumes of the Fundamentalism Project of the American Academy of Arts and Sciences, edited by Martin E. Marty and R. Scott Appleby: *Fundamentalisms Observed, Fundamentalisms and Society, Fundamentalisms and the State, Accounting for Fundamentalisms*, and *Fundamentalisms Comprehended* (Chicago: University of Chicago Press, 1991–5).
2 Gail Corrington Streete, *The Strange Woman: Power and Sex in the Bible* (Louisville, KY: Westminster John Knox, 1997), pp. 7, 8, 16, 62.
3 I use the word "tribe" to refer to intense, self-enclosed groups based on their real or presumed coherence along religious, racial, ethnic, ideological, or class lines, well aware that such usage may be an invention of modern anthropologists and then imposed on groups that may not refer to themselves in such terms. See, for example, the usage in Harold Isaacs, *Idols of the Tribe: Group Identity and Political Change* (New York: Harper and Row, 1975). The present use is closer to that of Eugen Rosenstock-Huessy, who speaks of the tribe – the reference group more extended than the family – as "a couche of values," a matrix, a womb. See Eugen Rosenstock-Huessy, *I Am an Impure Thinker* (Four Wells, VT: Argo, 1969).

4   William Blair Gould, *Frankl: Life with Meaning* (Pacific Grove, CA: Brooks/ Cole, 1993), pp. 120–1.

5   Georg Simmel, "The Stranger," in *The Sociology of Georg Simmel*, trans. Kurt H. Wolff (New York: Free Press, 1950), pp. 402–9.

6   Ibid, pp. 402, 406.

7   Conrad Richter, *A Simple Honorable Man* (New York: Knopf, 1962).

8   Lewis A. Coser, *The Functions of Social Conflict* (New York: Free Press, 1956).

9   Eric Hoffer, *The True Believer* (New York: Mentor, n.d.), p. 86.

10 Coser, *The Functions of Social Conflict*, pp. 39, 55.

11 Bronislaw Malinowski, "An Anthropological Analysis of War," in *Magic, Science, and Religion* (Glencoe, IL: Free Press, 1948), p. 285.

12 Quoted by Coser, *The Functions of Social Conflict*, pp. 104, 111.

13 Coser, *The Functions of Social Conflict*, pp. 129, 132.

14 Coser, *The Functions of Social Conflict*, p. 67; Max Scheler, "Das Ressentiment im Aufbau der Moralen," in *Vom Umsturz der Werte*, vol. 1 (Leipzig: Der Neue Geist Verlag, 1928), p. 89, quoted by Coser, *The Functions of Social Conflict*, p. 70.

15 Coser, *The Functions of Social Conflict*, p. 71.

Chapter 3 When Faith Communities Conflict

1   *British Social Attitudes: Cumulative Sourcebook* (Brookfield, VT: Gower, 1992); statistics on English and other scenes in the paragraphs that follow are taken from Stephen V. Monsma and J. Christopher Soper (eds.), *The Challenge of Pluralism: Church and State in Five Democracies* (Lanham, MD: Rowman & Littlefield, 1997), in this case, pp. 122–3.

2   Gerhard Robbers, "State and Church in Germany," in Gerhard Robbers (ed.), *State and Church in the European Union* (Baden-Baden: Nomos Verlagsgesellschaft, 1996), p. 60; see Monsma and Soper, *The Challenge of Pluralism*, p. 157.

3   *Statistical Yearbook, 1996* (The Hague: Central Bureau of Statistics, 1996), p. 53; see Monsma and Soper, *The Challenge of Pluralism*, p. 53.

4   Rod Dreher, "On Tiptoe through the Tulips," *National Review* (July 15, 2002), p. 30.

5   Peter Bentley, Tricia Blombery, and Philip J. Hughes, *A Yearbook for Australian Churches: 1994* (Melbourne: Christian Research Association, 1993), in Monsma and Soper, *The Challenge of Pluralism*, p. 88.

6   *The Economist*, November 2, 2003, pp. 3–4 in a supplement entitled "The Longest Journey."

7   Quoted in George Pellew, *John Jay* (Boston, MA: Houghton Mifflin, 1897), p. 79.

8   Edward Mead Earle (ed.), *The Federalist, etc.* (Washington, DC: Robert B. Luce, Ind., 1976), p. 9.

9   Edward Millican, *One United People: The Federalist Papers and the National Idea* (Lexington: University of Kentucky Press, 1990), p. 67.

10 These references are from a letter to James Parker, March 20, 1751, and "Increase of Mankind," quoted in David Freeman Hawke, *Franklin* (New York: Harper & Row, 1976), p. 95.

11 Robert Booth Fowler, *Unconventional Partners: Religion and Liberal Culture in the United States* (Grand Rapids, MI: William B. Eerdmans, 1989), pp. 4–5.

12 John Dewey, *A Common Faith* (New Haven, CT: Yale University Press, 1934).

13 Jeff Spinner-Halev, *Surviving Diversity: Religion and Democratic Citizenship* (Baltimore, MD: Johns Hopkins University Press, 2000), pp. 11–16, 17–19.

14 Spinner-Halev, *Surviving Diversity*, pp. 20, 23.

15 Spinner-Halev, *Surviving Diversity*, p. 96

16 Harold V. Bennett, *Injustice Made Legal: Deuteronomic Law and the Plight of Widows, Strangers, and Orphans in Ancient Israel* (Grand Rapids, MI: William B. Eerdmans, 2002), pp. 38–48; this quotation is from pp. 45ff.

17 Bennett, *Injustice Made Legal*, p. 153.

18 Bennett, *Injustice Made Legal*, p. 162, quoting Gordon W. Allport, *The Nature of Prejudice* (Reading, MA: Addison-Wesley, 1990), p. 444.

19 Bennett, *Injustice Made Legal*, pp. 165–71.

20 Marshall D. Sahlins and Elman R. Service, *Evolution and Culture* (Ann Arbor: University of Michigan Press, 1960); David Kaplan wrote the fourth chapter, from which this quotation is taken, p. 74.

21 Jeffrey Stout, *The Flight from Authority: Religion, Morality, and the Quest for Autonomy* (Notre Dame, IN: University of Notre Dame Press, 1981), p. 258.

22 Lonnie Kliever, Moral Education in a Pluralistic World, *Journal of the American Academy of Religion* 50: 1 (spring, 1992), p. 119.

23 Khaled Abou El Fadl et al., *The Place of Tolerance in Islam* (Boston, MA: Beacon Press, 2002); quotations are from pp. 4. 6, 8, 18, 19, 27–30, 32, 35, 37, 41, 44–8, 51, 55, 89.

24 Jacob Neusner, "Shalom: Complementarity," in *Jews and Christians: The Myth of a Common Tradition* (Philadelphia, PA: Trinity Press International, 1991), p. 107.

25 Stephen R. Barton, "Paul and the Limits of Tolerance," in Graham N. Stanton and Guy G. Stroumsa (eds.), *Tolerance and Intolerance in Early Judaism and Christianity* (Cambridge: Cambridge University Press, 1998), p. 131.

26 Reinhold Niebuhr, *The Children of Light and the Children of Darkness* (New York: Charles Scribner's Sons, 1945), p. 93.

Chapter 4 The Pluralist Polity

1   Robert Kane, *Through the Maze: Searching for Absolute Values in a Pluralistic World* (New York: Paragon House, 1994), p. 142.

2   James B. Wiggins, *In Praise of Religious Diversity* (New York: Routledge, 1996). I have drawn on Wiggins for several citations from authors with whom he carries on a conversation, as will be evident later.

3   Bernard Crick, *In Defense of Politics* (Baltimore, MD: Penguin Books, 1964), pp. 141, 15.

4   *World* (April 12, 2003), p. 5.

5   John G. Francis, "The Evolving Regulatory Structure of European Church–State Relationships," *Journal of Church and State* 34 (1992), p. 782.

6   Quoted in William Lee Miller, *The First Liberty: Religion and the American Republic* (New York: Knopf, 1986), p. 112.

7   Julián Marías, *Generations: A Historical Method*, trans. Harold C. Raley (Tuscaloosa: University of Alabama Press, 1970), p. 81.

8   Abdulaziz Sachedina, *The Islamic Roots of Democratic Pluralism* (New York: Oxford University Press, 2001), p. 424.

9   Sachedina, *The Islamic Roots of Democratic Pluralism*, p. 139.

10 Robert Spencer, *Islam Unveiled: Disturbing Questions about the World's Fastest-Growing Faith* (San Francisco, CA: Encounter Books, 2002), pp. vii, 176.

11 John Horton, "Toleration as a Virtue," in David Heyd, *Toleration: An Elusive Virtue* (Princeton, NJ: Princeton University Press, 1996), p. 28.

12 Morton Borden, *Jews, Turks, and Infidels* (Chapel Hill: University of North Carolina Press, 1984), p. 15; the Jefferson quote is from volume 1 of Paul L. Ford (ed.), *The Writings of Thomas Jefferson*, 12 vols. (New York: G. P. Putnam's, 1904–5), p. 71.

13 Borden, *Jews, Turks, and Infidels*, p. 91; the words appeared in *The Occident*, December, 1857, three years after a controversy over wording in a treaty.

14 *Christian Century* 68 (June 15, 1951), pp. 701–3.

15 Will Herberg, *Protestant, Catholic, Jew* (Garden City, NY: Doubleday, 1955).

16 John Courtney Murray, *We Hold These Truths: Catholic Reflections on the American Proposition* (New York: Sheed & Ward, 1960), pp. 15, 16, 17, 23–4.

17 Paul Mozjes, "The What and How of Dialogue," in M. Darrol Bryant and Frank Flinn (eds.), *Interreligious Dialogue: Voices from a New Frontier* (New York: Paragon House, 1989), p. 203; quoted by Wiggins, *In Praise of Religious Diversity*, p. 75.

18 *USA Today* (February 7, 2003), p. 13A.

19 *Chicago Tribune* (December 4, 2003), p. 29.

20 *Economist* (October 25, 2003), p. 45.

Notes

21 *New York Times* (October 1, 2003), p. A4.
22 Burton Bollag, "Muslims Worry French Universities," *Chronicle of Higher Education* (December 12, 2003), pp. A37–9.
23 Elaine Sciolino, "Ban Religious Attire in School, French Panel Says," *New York Times* (December 12, 2003), pp. A1, A17.

Chapter 5 Living with a Pluralist Polity

1 Mark Chaves and Philip S. Gorski, "Religious Pluralism and Religious Participation," *Annual Review of Sociology* 27: 26–81 (2001), pp. 261, 278ff.
2 Georg Simmel, "Conflict," in *The Sociology of Georg Simmel*, trans. Kurt H. Wolff (New York: Free Press, 1950), pp. 43–8.
3 Simmel, "Faithfulness and Gratitude" in *The Sociology of Georg Simmel*, trans. Kurt H. Wolff (New York: Free Press, 1950), pp. 383–4.
4 Lewis A. Coser, *The Functions of Social Conflict* (New York: Free Press, 1956), p. 71.
5 Robert J. Lifton, *Boundaries: Psychological Man in Revolution* (New York: Vintage, 1969), pp. 37, 43.
6 Edward Mead Earle (ed.), *The Federalist, etc.* (Washington, DC: Robert B. Luce, Ind., 1976), pp. 54, 61, 62, 339–41.
7 Kent Greenawalt, *Religious Convictions and Political Choice* (New York: Oxford University Press, 1988), pp. 149–52.
8 Louis Henkin, "Morals and the Constitution: The Sin of Obscenity," *Columbia Law Review* (1963), p. 441.
9 Basil Mitchell, *Law, Morality, and Religion in a Secular Society* (Oxford: Oxford University Press, 1967), p. 100.
10 Greenawalt, *Religious Convictions and Political Choice*, p. 53.
11 http://www.sttheodore.org/visit/html.

Chapter 6 The Risk of Hospitality

1 David Tracy, "Christianity in the Wider Context: Demands and Transformations," *Religion and Intellectual Life*, p. 12; quoted by James B. Wiggins, *In Praise of Religious Diversity* (New York: Routledge, 1996), p. 92.
2 Gabriel Marcel, *Creative Fidelity*, trans. Robert Rosthal (New York: Crossroad, 1982), pp. 211, 219.
3 Johannes P. Lous and Eugene A. Nida, *Greek–English Lexicon of the New Testament Based on Semantic Domains* (New York: United Bible Societies, 1988, 1989.)

4 Darrell Fasching, "Beyond Absolutism and Relativism: The Utopian Promise of Babel," *The Ellul Forum*, January 1994, Issue 12, Department of Religious Studies, University of South Florida, Tampa, FL, p. 9. Quoted by Wiggins, *In Praise of Religious Diversity*, p. 7.

5 Daniel J. Wakin, "Christian Charity, But for a Mosque?"*New York Times* (February 4, 2003), p. A32.

6 John Koenig, *New Testament Hospitality: Partnership with Strangers as Promise and Mission* (Philadelphia, PA: Fortress Press, 1985), pp. 1ff., 4ff., 7–10. Koenig provided some of the biblical references on the pages that follow.

7 Parker Palmer, *The Company of Strangers: Christians and the Renewal of America's Public Life* (New York: Crossroad, 1981), p. 69.

8 Philip Hallie, "From Cruelty to Goodness," *Hastings Center Report 11* (1981), pp. 26–7. See also his *Lest Innocent Blood Be Shed: The Story of the Village of Le Chambon and How Goodness Happened There* (San Francisco, CA: Harper & Row, 1980).

9 Martin E. Marty, Larry Greenfield, and David E. Guinn, *Religion and Public Discourse* (Chicago: Park Ridge Center, 1998). The report is no longer available; I will draw on it sufficiently that readers can get the gist.

10 Avishai Margalit, "The Ring: On Religious Pluralism;" see David Heyd, *Toleration: An Elusive Virtue* (Princeton, NJ: Princeton University Press, 1996), p. 147.

Chapter 7 Theological Integrity in Response

1 Nicholas Rescher, *Pluralism: Against the Demand for Consensus* (Oxford: Clarendon Press, 1993).

2 Peter Burke, *Varieties of Cultural History* (Ithaca, NY: Cornell University Press, 1997), p. 208.

3 Rescher, *Pluralism*, pp. 80, 125ff.

4 Raimundo Pannikar, "Religious Pluralism: The Metaphysical Challenge," in Leroy S. Rouner (ed.), *Religious Pluralism* (Notre Dame, IN: University of Notre Dame Press, 1984), p. 98.

5 George Santayana, *Reason in Religion*, quoted in Clifford Geertz, *The Interpretation of Cultures* (New York: Basic Books, 1973), p. 87.

6 John B. Cobb, Jr., "The Meaning of Pluralism for Christian Self-Understanding," in Leroy S. Rouner (ed.), *Religious Pluralism* (Notre Dame, IN: University of Notre Dame Press, 1984), pp. 165, 176.

7 Walter Lippmann, *A Preface to Morals* (New York: Macmillan, 1929), p. 76.

8 For searching analysis of proselytism from Islamic, Jewish, and Christian viewpoints, see John Witte, Jr. and Richard C. Martin (eds.), *Sharing the*

Books: Religious Perspectives on the Rights and Wrongs of Proselytism (Maryknoll, NY: Orbis, 1999). My introduction anticipates and summarizes the arguments (pp. 1–14).

9   E. Luther Copeland, *A New Meeting of the Religions: Interreligious Relationships and Theological Questioning* (Waco, TX: Baylor University Press, 1999), pp. 102–5. He cites John V. Taylor, "The Theological Basis of Interfaith Dialogue," in John Hick and Brian Hebblethwaite (eds.), *Christianity and Other Religions: Selected Readings* (Philadelphia, PA: Fortress Press, 1980), pp. 221–7, and Lesslie Newbigin, *The Gospel in a Pluralist Society* (Grand Rapids, MI: William B. Eerdmans, 1989), p. 182.

10 John Taylor, *The Primal Vision* (Philadelphia, PA: Fortress Press, 1963), p. 26.

11 Copeland and others credit Alan Race for having proposed a typology featuring the first three; a number of theologians are concentrating on the "acceptance" model, as surveyed in Paul Knitter, *Introducing Theologies of Religions* (Maryknoll, NY: Orbis Books, 2002). See also Alan Race, *Christians and Religious Pluralism: Patterns in the Theology of Religions* (London: SCM Press, 1983), p. 139.

12 Gavin D'Costa, *The Meeting of Religions and the Trinity* (Maryknoll, NY: Orbis Books, 2000), p. 2.

13 Crane Brinton, "Many Mansions," *American Historical Review* 49 (January, 1964), p. 315.

14 John Horton and Susan Mendus (eds.), *After MacIntyre: Critical Perspectives on the World of Alasdair MacIntyre* (Cambridge: Polity Press, 1994), p. 3; also quoted by D'Costa, *The Meeting of Religions and the Trinity*, pp. 3ff. For the full argument, see Alasdair MacIntyre, *After Virtue*, 2nd edn. (London: Duckworth, 1985).

15 D'Costa, *The Meeting of Religions and the Trinity*, pp. 19–20.

16 Knitter, *Introducing Theologies of Religions*, p. 173; see also pp. 185–97, 224–37.

17 Timothy C. Tennent, *Christianity at the Religious Roundtable: Evangelicalism in Conversation with Hinduism, Buddhism, and Islam* (Grand Rapids, MI: Baker, 2002), pp. 9, 11, 26, 31–2.

18 Dan Cohn-Sherbok, *Judaism and Other Faiths* (New York: Macmillan, 1994), pp. 6, 5, 24, 163, 171. D'Costa, *The Meeting of Religions and the Trinity*, pp. 40–5, critiques these.

19 Paul Elmen, *The Restoration of Meaning to Contemporary Life* (Garden City, NY: Doubleday, 1958), p. 189.

20 Marc Gopin, *Holy War, Holy Peace: How Religion Can Bring Peace to the Middle East* (New York: Oxford University Press, 2002), pp. 198ff.

Index

189